2 More Grammar Practice

SECOND EDITION

MGrP Quiz (used (21-34)

LRc

HEINLE
CENGAGE Learning

Australia • Brazil • Japan • Korea • Mexico • Singapore • Spain • United Kingdom • United States

Contents

To the Teacher

The name says it all—*More Grammar Practice*.

More Grammar Practice has <u>more</u> to help English learners master essential grammar topics, whether you use it as a supplement to your grammar, reading, writing, or listening/speaking course or as a self-study supplement.

The grammar topics are organized in a two-page format to keep students focused on one grammar topic at a time.

The second edition of *More Grammar Practice* includes new editing exercises in which students use their knowledge of grammar to edit short texts such as Web pages, emails, dialogues, paragraphs, notes, and informational texts.

Features

Each two-page grammar topic contains:

- **Grammar Chart:** Each grammar chart presents a grammar topic in an easy-to-read chart with concise language and clear example sentences. The charts provide information about forms as well as usage. Additional **Language Notes** engage students with real-world applications of the targeted grammar topic.
- **Exercises:** Each grammar topic has ample opportunities for students to practice and review previous topics.

New to This Edition

- **Editing exercises** allow students to apply their knowledge of grammar while they practice editing skills. The editing texts reflect common ways people use English in their daily lives. Additionally, some of the editing texts are dialogues, which teachers can use for additional listening and speaking practice.
- **Online E-Book** offers an interactive approach to the charts and exercises from *More Grammar Practice*.
- **Answer key** is available from the Heinle Web site.

BASE FORM	–S FORM
I **love** animals.	My mother **loves** children.
We **love** animals.	My father **loves** children.
You **love** animals.	My family **loves** children.
My children **love** animals.	My dog **loves** children.
They **love** animals.	Everyone **loves** children.

Language Notes:
1. Use the –s form after *he, she, it*, singular nouns, *everyone, everybody, everything, someone, somebody, something, no one, nobody*, or *nothing*.
2. Add –es to verbs that end in *s, sh, tch, ch, x*, or *z*: wash → *washes*, touch → *touches*
3. Drop the –y and add –ies to most verbs that end in y: try → *tries*, carry → *carries*
4. Use the base form after *I, we, you, they*, and plural nouns.
5. Three verbs have an irregular –s form: have → *has*, go → *goes*, do → *does*. The verb *be* has three forms in the simple present tense: (*I*) *am*; (*you, we, they*) *are*; and (*he, she, it*) *is*.

■ **EXERCISE 1** Fill in the blank with the correct form of the <u>underlined</u> word.

Example I <u>work</u> in an office. My wife _____works_____ in a hospital.

1. We <u>write</u> the answers. The teacher ____writes____ the questions.

2. I <u>wash</u> the vegetables. My cousin ____washes____ the dishes.

3. My husband <u>speaks</u> Spanish. I ____speak____ Spanish too.

4. I <u>study</u> science. My sister ____studies____ math.

5. You <u>eat</u> a lot of meat. I ____eat____ a lot of vegetables.

6. She <u>cleans</u> the kitchen. He ____cleans____ the garage.

7. I <u>enjoy</u> my job. My friend ____enjoys____ his job too.

8. He <u>lives</u> alone. I ____live____ with my family.

9. I <u>go</u> to the bank every morning. My husband ____goes____ to his office.

10. My teacher <u>likes</u> the city. I ____like____ the country.

11. The bus driver <u>has</u> a nice smile. You ____have____ a nice smile too.

12. We <u>go</u> to the supermarket on Saturday. He ____goes____ to the supermarket on Thursday night.

13. You <u>walk</u> 2 miles to school. They ____walk____ 1 mile to school.

14. Eggs <u>break</u> easily. A glass also ____breaks____ easily.

EXERCISE 2 Fill in each blank in the paragraphs with the correct form of a word from the box. Use each word only one time.

Example My uncle ____owns____ a newspaper.

A.

| ~~own(s)~~ draw(s) speak(s) ask(s) make(s) write(s) do(es) |

Everyone in my family works at my uncle's newspaper. My brother and I are reporters. Every day we (1) _____ questions and (2) _____ news stories. My mother is the cartoonist. She (3) _____ funny pictures of people who are in the news. My father is in charge of advertising. He (4) _____ with companies that want to advertise in our paper. My aunt is the editor-in-chief. She (5) _____ the final decisions about the news stories. My uncle is the managing editor. Everyone (6) _____ what he says.

Handwritten answers:
A.
1. ask
2. write
3. draws
4. speaks
5. maks
6. does

B.

| work(s) close(s) come(s) go(es) buy(s) cook(s) become(s) open(s) |

My husband and I (1) _____ together at a small seafood restaurant. He is the cook. In the morning, he (2) _____ to the supermarket and (3) _____ the best fish and vegetables for that day's menu. Then he (4) _____ back to the restaurant and (5) _____ all the food for the day. We (6) _____ the restaurant at 11:00 a.m., and it quickly (7) _____ very busy. We (8) _____ the restaurant at 10:00 p.m.

Handwritten answers:
B
1. work
2. goes
3. buys
4. comes
5. kook
6. open
7. becomes
8. close

C.

| work(s) enjoy(s) come(s) tell(s) bring(s) examine(s) |

My wife is a doctor. All her patients are children. The parents (1) _____ their sick children to her. She (2) _____ the children and sometimes gives them medicine. My wife (3) _____ long hours, but she (4) _____ her job. When she (5) _____ home at night, we (6) _____ each other about our day.

Handwritten answers:
C.
1. bring
2. examines
3. works
4. enjoys
5. comes
6. tell

EXERCISE 3 Read the conversation and correct the mistakes. There are 10 mistakes.

Example Ricardo ~~get~~ gets up early.

Ricardo: Tomorrow ~~are~~ is Saturday. I love weekends.

Yolanda: Me too. I ~~likes~~ to rest.

Ricardo: Rest? Not me. On Saturdays, I ~~waking~~ up early and go to the gym.

Yolanda: Really? My sister, Alicia, ~~am~~ is like that. She ~~get~~ gets up early and go to the gym every morning. On Saturdays, I ~~am~~ sleep until noon.

Ricardo: My brother, Jorge, ~~like~~ is likes that. He stays up until 3:00 in the morning and sleeps late the next day.

Yolanda: Maybe you and I ~~am~~ are in the wrong families!

Forms of the Simple Present Tense **3**

Practice 2 — Negative Statements with the Simple Present Tense

EXAMPLE	EXPLANATION
My neighbors have two dogs. They **do not / don't have** a cat.	Use *do not* + the base form of the verb with *I, you, we, they*, or a plural noun.
My daughter wants a puppy. She **does not / doesn't want** a kitten.	Use *does not* + the base form of the verb with *he, she, it*, or a singular noun.

Language Notes: 1. *Don't* is the contraction for *do not. Doesn't* is the contraction for *does not.*
2. Always use the base form of the verb after *don't* and *doesn't.*

■ EXERCISE 1   Fill in the negative form of the underlined verb.

Example He <u>talks</u> loudly. We _____**don't talk**_____ loudly.

1. I <u>swim</u> very well. You ___*don't swim*___ very well.

2. He <u>listens</u> to the radio. She ___*doesn't listen*___ to the radio.

3. We <u>grow</u> tomatoes and peppers. They ___*don't grow*___ vegetables.

4. You <u>know</u> my brother. She ___*doesn't know*___ my family.

5. She <u>reads</u> many magazines. We ___*don't read*___ magazines.

6. I <u>watch</u> old TV shows. You ___*don't watch*___ reality shows.

7. They <u>do</u> their laundry. She ___*doesn't do*___ her laundry.

8. We <u>go</u> shopping at the mall. He ___*doesn't go*___ shopping.

9. The children <u>stay</u> home. The adults ___*don't stay*___ home.

10. He <u>has</u> four brothers. I ___*don't have*___ any brothers.

■ EXERCISE 2   Unscramble the words to make a correct sentence.

Example in the west / rise / the sun / doesn't

__The sun doesn't rise in the west.__

1. a lot of money / have / she / doesn't

   ___she doesn't have a lot of money___

2. like / he / to get up early / does / not

   ___He does not like to get up early.___

3. don't / they / want / a lot of money / to pay

   ___They don't want to pay a lot of money.___

4. he / does / walk to work / not

   ___He does not walk to work.___

5. not / put sugar / in her / does / my mother / tea

My mother does not Put sugar in her tea.

6. rain / every weekend / doesn't / it

It doesn't rain every weekend.

■ EXERCISE 3   Use a negative verb to answer the question.

Example   Why does he walk to work every day?

Because he (not / have) __does not have / doesn't have__ a car.

1. Will you join me for a cup of coffee?

No thanks. I (not / drink) _do not drink / don't drink_ coffee.

2. Why don't they laugh at my jokes?

They (not / like) _do not lik / don't like_ your sense of humor.

3. You look tired. Are you okay?

I (not / feel) _do not feel / don't feel_ very well. I think I'll lie down.

4. Who is that guy driving the red car?

Sorry, I (not / know) _do not know / don't know_ who he is.

5. Why doesn't Miguel come to the restaurant with us?

He (not / feel) _does not feel / doesn't feel_ well.

6. Can I borrow her pen?

She (not / have) _does not have / doesn't have_ a pen.

■ EXERCISE 4   Read the email and correct the mistakes. There are 7 mistakes.

Example   He ~~don't~~ (doesn't) like fast food.

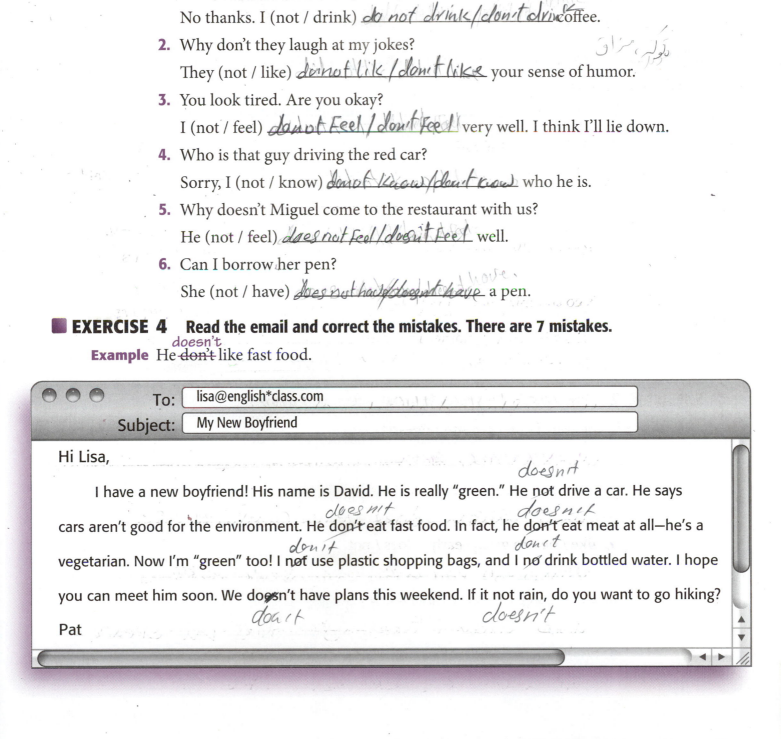

To: lisa@english*class.com

Subject: My New Boyfriend

Hi Lisa,

I have a new boyfriend! His name is David. He is really "green." He not drive _(doesn't)_ a car. He says

cars aren't good for the environment. He don't _(doesn't)_ eat fast food. In fact, he don't _(doesn't)_ eat meat at all—he's a

vegetarian. Now I'm "green" too! I not _(don't)_ use plastic shopping bags, and I no _(don't)_ drink bottled water. I hope

you can meet him soon. We doesn't _(don't)_ have plans this weekend. If it not rain _(doesn't)_, do you want to go hiking?

Pat

WH– WORD	DO / DOES DON'T / DOESN'T	SUBJECT	VERB	COMPLEMENT	SHORT ANSWER
		My friend	**has**	a dog.	
		She	**doesn't have**	a cat.	
	Does	she	**have**	a Labrador retriever?	Yes, she **does**. / No, she **doesn't**.
What kind of dog	**does**	she	**have**?		
Why	**doesn't**	she	**have**	a cat?	

EXERCISE 1 Unscramble the words to make a question. Put a question mark at the end of each question.

Example you / your lunch / buy / where / do

<u>**Where do you buy your lunch?**</u>

1. ask / do / so many questions / children / why

<u>Why do children ask so many question?</u>

2. do / this word / you / how / pronounce

<u>How do you Pronounce this word?</u>

3. money / we / where / change / do

<u>Where do we change money?</u>

4. how often / her email / check / does / she

<u>How often does she check her email?</u>

5. the children / of ice cream / what flavor / want / do

<u>What flavor of ice cream do the children want?</u>

6. does / how much / cost / this computer

<u>How much does this computer cost?</u>

7. need / who / to speak to / you / do

<u>Who do you need to speak to?</u>

8. he / languages / does / how many / speak

<u>How many languages does he speak?</u>

9. open / do / the banks / when

<u>When do the banks open?</u>

■ **EXERCISE 2** (Circle) the correct word to complete each sentence.

Example (Does) / Do he like pizza for lunch? ~~Rubenstein her tea.~~

1. Where / What do you keep the milk? ~~It doesn't rain every weekend.~~
2. When <u>does</u> / do he eat dinner?
3. Why (don't) / doesn't you like your meal?
4. (Does / Do) the baby use a spoon or a fork?
5. (Where) / What do they want to go?
6. Where do they goes / (go) for vacation?

■ **EXERCISE 3** Read the conversation and correct the mistakes. There are 7 mistakes.

Example Why ^don't you ~~not~~ go?

Karen:	What ^*do* you want to do tonight? ~~Does~~ *Do* you want to stay home or go out?
Tina:	Let's go out. I don't work tomorrow.
Karen:	Why you ^*don't* ~~not~~ work tomorrow?
Tina:	It's my day off. Hey! Tom is having a party. You do ^*do you* want to go?
Karen:	Where ^*does* do he lives?
Tina:	Just down the street. We can walk there.
Karen:	What time ^*does* the party starts?
Tina:	I think it starts at 7:00.
Karen:	Doesn't he has ^*have* a pool?
Tina:	Yes. It's a pool party.
Karen:	Great! Let's go to Tom's party!

Practice 4 Uses of the Simple Present Tense

EXAMPLE	USE
The sun **rises** in the east.	To state a fact
Marianne **comes** from Russia.	To show one's country, city, or place of origin
We **eat** dinner around 6:00 p.m.	To show a regular activity, a habit, or a custom

■ **EXERCISE 1** <u>Underline</u> the simple present tense verb in each sentence. Then write *fact*, *origin*, or *custom* beside each sentence to show the use of the verb.

Example Anna <u>comes</u> from Canada.   *origin*

1. The earth circles the sun.   *circles fact*
2. I <u>s</u>end email every day.   *send, custom*
3. Fish come from lakes and oceans.   *come fact/origin*
4. Fruit grows on trees.   *grows, fact*
5. She drinks eight glasses of water every day. _____
6. Elena comes from Chile.   _____
7. The magazine comes once a month.   _____
8. Paper comes from trees.   _____
9. You exercise every day.   _____
10. I go out to eat every Saturday.   _____
11. I speak to my mother every day.   _____
12. Eggs are from chickens.   _____
13. The moon is easy to see at night.   _____
14. The students are from Morocco.   _____
15. He cleans his apartment on Friday.   _____
16. Pollution comes from cars.   _____
17. My mother is from Guatemala.   _____

■ **EXERCISE 2** Write a simple present tense sentence about your daily activities and habits.

Example (in the morning) <u>I drink orange juice in the morning.</u>

1. (in the morning) _____
2. (at lunchtime) _____
3. (in the evening) _____

■ **EXERCISE 3**   **Read Marta's schedule and answer each question.**

Example   What does Marta do on Saturdays?   ~~*[handwritten]*~~

<u>Marta goes shopping on Saturdays.</u>

> **Name:** Marta Vasquez
> **City, Province, and Country of origin:** Toronto, Ontario, Canada
> **Activities:**   **Facts about me:**
> ● Jogs—Mondays, Wednesdays, and Fridays   ● tall
> ● Plays basketball—Tuesdays and Thursdays   ● athletic
> ● Goes shopping—Saturdays   ● two brothers

1. When does Marta jog?
   He jogs on Mondays, Wednesday and Fridays.

2. What does Marta do on Tuesdays?
   Marta plays basketball on Tuesdays

3. Is Marta short?
   No he isn't, he is tall.

4. Does Marta have two sisters?
   No he doesn't have two sisters.

5. Where is Marta from?
   He is from Canada.

■ **EXERCISE 4**   **Read the email and correct the mistakes. There are 7 mistakes.**

Example   Our teacher ~~come~~ *comes* from California.

> **To:** bill98@english*class.com
> **Subject:** Soccer?
>
> Hi Bill!
>
> Guess what! We has a new exchange student in my class. His name is Min-ho, and he come
> from Korea. Actually, he come from Seoul. Seoul are the capital of Korea. He play soccer really well.
> We plays soccer together every day after school. Do you want to play soccer with us this weekend?
> We plays at Riverside Park every Sunday. I hope I will see you there!
> Mark

Practice 5 — Frequency Words and Position of Frequency Words.

FREQUENCY WORD		EXAMPLE
always	100%	The sun **always** rises in the east.
usually / generally	↑	Children **usually** / **generally** like to watch cartoons.
often / frequently		Parents **often** / **frequently** read to their children.
sometimes / occasionally		Rivers **sometimes** / **occasionally** flood after it rains.
rarely / seldom / hardly ever	↓	It **rarely** / **seldom** / **hardly ever** rains in the desert.
never / not ever	0%	The sun **never** rises / does**n't ever** rise in the west.

Language Notes:
1. Frequency words usually come after the verb *be* but before other verbs.
2. The following frequency words can also come at the beginning of a sentence: *usually, generally, often, frequently, sometimes, occasionally.*
   Often, frequently, and *occasionally* can also come at the end of a sentence.
3. In questions or negative sentences, frequency words usually come before the main verb.
4. Use *how often* in a *wh-* question if the answer is a frequency word or phrase:
   How often do you wash the floor?
   I *rarely* wash the floor.

■ EXERCISE 1   Rewrite the sentence with the frequency words in parentheses.

Example My sister calls me. (hardly ever)

My sister hardly *ever* calls me.

1. My best friend and I eat lunch together. (frequently)

   My best friend and I frequently eat lunch together.

2. The banks are open on Sundays. (never)

   The banks are never open on Sundays.

3. The post office is closed on holidays. (always)

   The Post office is always closed on holidays.

4. We like to go to the park and feed the pigeons. (occasionally)

   We occasionally like to go to the Park and feed the Pigeons.

5. He stays up very late the night before an exam. (generally)

   He generally stays up very late the night before an exam.

6. The mail comes in the afternoon. (usually)

   The mail usually comes in the afternoon.

■ EXERCISE 2   Unscramble the words and write a correct statement or question. If there is a question mark, make the sentence a question.

Example usually / eat / a big breakfast / I

I usually *eat a big breakfast.*

1. check / you / how often / your voice mail / do

   How often do you check your voice mail ?

2. in the evenings / hardly ever / my roommates / at home / are

   My roommates hardly ever at home in the evenings

3. he / out of town for the weekend / goes / usually

   He usually goes out of town for the weekend.

4. the population of the world / how often / double / in size / does

   How often does the population of the world double in size?

5. late / sometimes / is / this bus

   Some times this bus is late. (sometimes?)

■ **EXERCISE 3**   **Answer each question using a frequency word.**

Example How often do you drink soda? <u>I seldom drink soda.</u>

1. Do you ever go to the beach in December?

   I occasionally go to the beach in December

2. How often do your friends call you?

   Sometimes my friends call me.

3. Is the weather here ever cloudy?

   Yes the weather is very cloudy.

■ **EXERCISE 4**   **Read the email and correct the mistakes. There are 7 mistakes.**

Example I ~~walk always~~ with my neighbor.   _always walk_

To: reem@english*class.com

Subject: Farmer's Market

Dear Reem,

   I love my new neighborhood! There's a farmer's market near my apartment. Lots of fresh fruits and vegetables always are for sale. I go every generally Saturday. My neighbor comes sometimes with me. We walk usually there, but we take occasionally the bus if it's raining. After the farmer's market, my neighbor and I make frequently lunch with the food we bought. Always we love the market and our lunches together.

Simon

Frequency Words and Position of Frequency Words   **11**

SIMPLE PRESENT FORM	PRESENT CONTINUOUS FORM
She sometimes **wears** a dress.	She**'s wearing** sunglasses right now.
She **doesn't wear** shorts.	She **isn't wearing** shorts today.
Does she ever **wear** a bathing suit?	**Is** she **wearing** a T-shirt now?
Yes, she **does**. / No, she **doesn't**.	Yes, she **is**. / No, she **isn't**.
How often **does** she **wear** a dress?	What **is** she **wearing** today?
Why **doesn't** she ever **wear** a bathing suit?	Why **isn't** she **wearing** shoes right now?

SIMPLE PRESENT TENSE	EXPLANATION
Plants **need** water in order to live.	Use the simple present tense to talk about a
We **do** our homework in the evening.	general truth, a habitual activity, or a custom.
People **cook** rice in a variety of ways.	

PRESENT CONTINUOUS TENSE	EXPLANATION
They **are studying**.	Use the present continuous tense for an action
I**'m using** a workbook in my English class.	that is in progress at this moment or for a longer action that is in progress at this general time.

■ **EXERCISE 1**   (Circle) all of the simple present verbs. <u>Underline</u> all of the present continuous verbs.

Examples My sister (visits) me on Monday. Today she <u>is visiting</u> friends.

A. (1) My older brother (works) as a reporter for the largest newspaper in my country. (2) He (writes) about international news. (3) It (is) a good job. (4) He and his family (move) to a new country every year. (5) Right now they<u>'re living</u> in Jerusalem. (6) His wife and children <u>are learning</u> Arabic and Hebrew, (7) but my brother already (speaks) these languages. (8) He (speaks) four languages. (9) He <u>is learning</u> Spanish (10) because he (wants) to travel in South America.

B. (1) My younger brother (is) a student. (2) He's <u>studying</u> business at the university in my hometown. (3) He (works) at a couple of part-time jobs <u>during</u> the school year. (4) He (likes) to try different jobs. (5) Right now, he's <u>waiting</u> tables at a restaurant in the evenings. (6) Also, he is <u>managing</u> a car (wash) on the weekends.

■ **EXERCISE 2**   Fill in the correct form of the verb in parentheses. Use the simple present or the present continuous tense.

Examples She (like) _____ **likes** _____ to watch TV at night.

He (talk) _____ **is talking** _____ on the phone right now.

1. He (sleep) _____ *is sleeping* _____ right now. Please call back later.

2. She always (type) _____ types _____ her letters to her parents.

3. We (sit) _____ are sitting _____ in the best seats for this concert.

4. You (talk) _____ are talking _____ all the time.

5. Please be quiet! I (watch) _____ am watching _____ a good movie.

6. My mother and I (shop) _____ shop _____ at the mall each month.

7. My friends (sing) _____ are singing _____ at the concert today.

8. It (rain) _____ is raining _____ right now.

9. Brendan (play) _____ plays _____ soccer with Sanjit on Tuesday.

10. Susannah (wash) _____ washes _____ her hair every morning.

■ **EXERCISE 3   Read the email and correct the mistakes. There are 7 mistakes.**

Example   It ~~being~~ ^{is} summer.

To: mami@home*france.com

Subject: Park

Dear Grandma,

It is finally springtime here in Missouri. I sit [I'm sitting] in the park right now with my laptop. It is being a beautiful day. The birds are sing [singing], and flowers are blooming. Children is [are] playing together in the grass.

This is my favorite park. I am liking to walk along the paths. Sometimes I watching [watch] people fish in the lake. On Sundays, I usually am bringing [I am... bring] my lunch and stay all afternoon.

I wish you could see this park, Grandma. It's a very special place.

I miss you!

Your grandson,

Christophe

Contrasting the Simple Present Tense and the Present Continuous Tense   **13**

ACTION VERBS	NONACTION VERBS
Carmen **is living** in Osaka, Japan, this year. She **is studying** Japanese.	She **likes** her new life. She **doesn't understand** much yet. She **hears** some of the words clearly.

Language Notes:

1. We do not usually use the present continuous tense with certain verbs called nonaction verbs. These verbs describe a state or a condition, not an action. We use the simple present tense, even when we talk about right now.

2. Some nonaction verbs are:

be	hear	mean	see
believe	know	need	seem
care	like	own	think
cost	love	prefer	understand
have	matter	remember	want

3. *Think, have*, and the sense perception verbs (*look, taste, feel, smell*) can be both action and nonaction verbs, but the meaning is different.

■ **EXERCISE 1**   Underline the nonaction verbs in the diary entry. (There are 21 nonaction verbs.)

Example I <u>have</u> many letters to write.

Dear Diary,

   I <u>think</u> I really <u>like</u> my life in Japan! I <u>like</u> my host parents, Mr. and Mrs. Yamada. They <u>are</u> very kind, and

they <u>care</u> for me like a daughter. I <u>like</u> my room, and I <u>love</u> the house.

   I'm learning Japanese, but I <u>don't understand</u> what people are saying in conversations yet. I often

<u>need</u> my dictionary. I look up many words every day. Sometimes I <u>understand</u> the words, but

I <u>don't know</u> what they <u>mean</u>.

   When Mrs. Yamada suggests that we do something together, I <u>wonder</u>, "Does she <u>want</u> me to do it?"

Everything <u>seems</u> so confusing. I <u>need</u> help! Sometimes I <u>prefer</u> to stay in my room because that <u>seems</u>

easy. But I <u>believe</u> that hard work <u>matters</u> most.

Carmen

■ EXERCISE 2   Circle the correct tense of the underlined verbs.

Example He is wanting /(wants) to meet famous movie stars.

Dear Diary,

Life (1) is getting / gets better here in Osaka. My Japanese (2) is improving / improves every day.

I (3) have / am having two new friends, Erika and Satoko. They (4) are helping / help me with my language

and culture questions. I (5) am wanting / want to invite them to visit me when I go back to Texas. They

(6) are seeming / seem easy to talk to, and they both (7) are having / have a great sense of humor.

I (8) am liking / like to go shopping. Everything (9) is costing / costs more here, so I usually just

(10) am looking / look in the shop windows. I (11) am hearing / hear a lot of Japanese conversations when I

am in the shops, and I (12) am understanding / understand about 40 percent of them. I'm a little shy, and I

(13) am preferring / prefer just to listen and not to speak right now. Erika and Satoko sometimes

(14) are going / go with me and (15) are translating / translate for me.

Carmen

■ EXERCISE 3   Read the paragraph and correct the mistakes. There are 9 mistakes.

Example We is hearing the wonderful music on the radio.
$\qquad\qquad\qquad$ *hear*

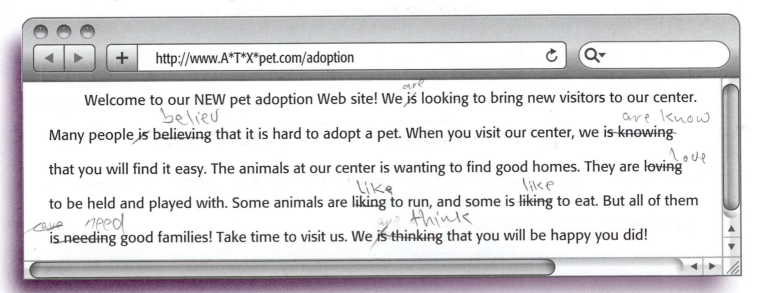

Welcome to our NEW pet adoption Web site! We is looking to bring new visitors to our center.

Many people is believing that it is hard to adopt a pet. When you visit our center, we is knowing

that you will find it easy. The animals at our center is wanting to find good homes. They are loving

to be held and played with. Some animals are liking to run, and some is liking to eat. But all of them

is needing good families! Take time to visit us. We is thinking that you will be happy you did!

Questions with the Simple Present Tense and the Present Continuous Tense

QUESTIONS WITH THE SIMPLE PRESENT TENSE

WH– WORD	DO OR DOES (+ N'T)	SUBJECT	MAIN VERB	COMPLEMENT
		She	**watches**	TV.
When	**does**	she	**watch**	TV?
		My parents	**speak**	English.
What language	**do**	your parents	**speak**?	
		Your sister	**lives**	with roommates.
With whom	**does**	she	**live**?	
Who	**does**	she	**live**	with?
		You	**don't like**	her roommate.
Why	**don't**	you	**like**	her roommate?

QUESTIONS WITH THE PRESENT CONTINUOUS TENSE

WH– WORD	BE (+ N'T)	SUBJECT	BE	VERB + ING	COMPLEMENT
		She	**is**	**sitting**	in her room.
Where	**is**	she		**sitting**?	
		You	**aren't**	**listening**	to the music.
Why	**aren't**	you		**listening**	to the music?

■ **EXERCISE 1**   Match each question to the correct answer in the second column.

1. ___a___ Are you speaking to me?   **a.** Yes, I am.

2. ___f___ Do you want to eat now?   **b.** At about 11:00 p.m.

3. ___c___ What is your name?   **c.** Yumiko Toshimo.

4. ___j___ How long is the movie?   **d.** Fine, thanks.

5. ___b___ When do you go to sleep?   **e.** No, he isn't.

6. ___h___ How old is she?   **f.** Yes, I do.

7. ___e___ Is he a doctor?   **g.** He is tired.

8. ___g___ Why is he sleeping?   **h.** Almost 19.

9. ___d___ How are you feeling?   **i.** No, you're not.

10. ___i___ Am I bothering you?   **j.** About two hours.

■ **EXERCISE 2**   Find the mistakes in the <u>underlined</u> portions of each question. Then rewrite the question correctly. If there are no mistakes, write *correct*.

Examples <u>Is</u> he <u>speak</u> to his parents?

   Is he speaking to his parents?

   <u>Do</u> you <u>want</u> to come to my house?

   correct

1. <u>Do</u> she <u>visiting</u> her friends in Japan this week?

    Is she visiting her friends in Japan this week?

2. <u>Are</u> they <u>live</u> in Mexico?

    Do the live in Mexico?

3. <u>Is</u> she <u>teaching</u> her afternoon class today?

    Correct

4. <u>Are</u> you <u>wear</u> glasses every day?

    Do you wear glasses every day?

■ EXERCISE 3   Use the words in parentheses to write a question.

Example I'm not watching TV tonight. (why)

<u>**Why aren't you watching TV tonight?**</u>

1. I am flying to São Paulo. (where)

    Where are you flying?

2. Steve does his homework. (when)

    When does steve do his homework

3. They need to go to the dentist. (why)

    Why do the need to go to the dentist?

■ EXERCISE 4   Read the conversation and correct the mistakes. There are 5 mistakes.

Example When ~~does~~ *do* you go to school?

Olivia:	What language *do* your grandparents speak?
Emma:	They speak Spanish. Why ~~does~~ *do* you want to know?
Olivia:	I am just curious. My grandparents speak German.
Emma:	When *are* ~~is~~ you going to visit them?
Olivia:	I am not going to visit them this year.
Emma:	Why isn't *aren't* you going?
Olivia:	My grandparents are traveling back to Germany.
Emma:	When does they leave?
Olivia:	They leave next week.

Practice 9   Future Tense with *Will*

EXAMPLE	EXPLANATION
In the future, people **will live** longer. They **will need** help from their children.	We use *will* + the base form of the verb to form the future tense.
I**'ll be** 55 years old in 2050. You**'ll help** your parents.	We can contract *will* with the subject pronouns: *I'll, you'll, he'll, she'll, it'll, we'll, they'll.*
The population **will not decrease**. I **won't live** with my children.	To form the negative, put *not* after *will*. The contraction for *will not* is *won't*.
QUESTION FORM	**SHORT ANSWER**
Will she **live** with her son?	Yes, she **will**. / No, she **won't**.
Where will she **live**? **Why won't** she **live** alone?	

■ EXERCISE 1   Use the contraction of *will* ('*ll*) with the subject pronoun or *will not* (*won't*) to complete each statement.

Example (I / not / get) _____I won't get_____ on the bus at 7:30 a.m.

1. (I / call) _____I'll call_____ you when I arrive in the city.
2. (He / not / be) ___He won't be___ at the bus station.
3. (You / not / need) ___You won't need___ any money for the taxi.
4. (You / buy) ___You'll buy___ a house one day.
5. (She / meet) ___She'll meet___ you on the street corner.
6. (They / not / like) ___They won't like___ the menu in the cafeteria.
7. (We / not / go) ___We won't go___ if it rains tomorrow.
8. (It / be) ___It'll be___ cloudy in the morning.
9. (It / not / rain) ___It won't rain___ tomorrow.
10. (I / walk) Tomorrow ___I'll walk Tomorrow___ 5 miles.
11. (she / not / play) Tonight ___she won't play___ basketball.
12. (I / not / look) ___I won't look___ at my present until the party.
13. (He / be) ___He'll be___ ready for the game.
14. (We / listen) ___We'll listen___ to the music at the concert.

■ EXERCISE 2   Write a question using *will* and the words in parentheses.

Example (Why / you / not / be) _____Why won't you be_____ here tomorrow?

1. (Where / you / go) ___Where you will go___ to college?

2. (How long / they / study) ~~How long they will~~ ^study English?

3. (Why / she / not / finish) ~~Why won't she finish~~ that book?

4. (Whom / he / go) ~~Whom will he go~~ to the concert with?

5. (When / you / see) ~~When you will see~~ your family?

6. (What / you / do) ~~What will you do~~ this weekend?

7. (Why / not / you / eat) ~~Why won't you eat~~ the fish?

8. (How long / he / try) ~~How long will he try~~ to get that job?

9. (Where / she / keep) ~~Where will she keep~~ her new dog?

10. (When / it / be) ~~When will it be~~ nice to visit?

■ **EXERCISE 3** **Read the email and correct the mistakes. There are 6 mistakes.**

Example People ~~did~~ ^will eat seafood tomorrow.

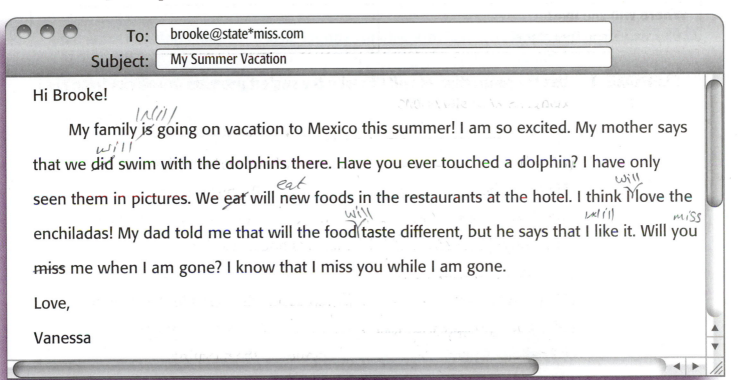

To: brooke@state*miss.com

Subject: My Summer Vacation

Hi Brooke!

My family ~~is~~ ^will going on vacation to Mexico this summer! I am so excited. My mother says

that we ~~did~~ ^will swim with the dolphins there. Have you ever touched a dolphin? I have only

seen them in pictures. We ~~eat~~ will ^eat new foods in the restaurants at the hotel. I think I^will love the

enchiladas! My dad told me that will the food taste different, but he says that I like it. Will you

~~miss~~ ^miss me when I am gone? I know that I miss you while I am gone.

Love,

Vanessa

Practice 10 Future Tense with *Be going to*

EXAMPLE	EXPLANATION
People **are going to live** longer. They **are going to need** help from their children.	We use *be going to* + the base form of the verb to form the future tense.
I'**m not going to live** with my children.	To form the negative, put *not* after the form of *be* or contracted form.
QUESTION FORM	**SHORT ANSWER**
Is she **going to live** with her son?	Yes, she **is**. / No, she **isn't**.
Where is she **going to live**? **Why isn't** she **going to live** with her son?	

■ **EXERCISE 1** Complete the sentence with the correct form of *be* (*not*) *going to* + the base form of the verb.

Example He (go) _____is going to go_____ to school in the fall.

1. Many students (go) _are going to go_ to the lecture about politics.
2. Paul (not / study) _Paul is not going to study_ tonight.
3. Evelyn (not / stay) _Evelyn is not going to stay_ at home tonight.
4. The department store (be) _is going to be_ busy all day.
5. The children (play) _are going to play_ games at the party.
6. Many kids (play) _are going to play_ football next weekend.
7. I (walk) _am / 'm going to walk_ into town.
8. Everybody (sleep) _is / 's going to sleep_ well tonight.
9. She (not / travel) _is / 's not going to travel_ during the winter vacation.
10. We (not / worry) _are / 're not going to worry_ about our test grades.

■ **EXERCISE 2** Unscramble the words and phrases. Some sentences are statements. Some are questions.

Example going to / into a larger apartment / she / is / move

She is going to move into a larger apartment.

1. finish / you / soon / college / going to / are

   Your going to finish soon college.

2. wake up / for class on time / we / going to / are

   Are we going to wake up for class ontime ?

3. I'm / any more money / spend / going to / not

   I'm not going to spend more many .

4. why / eat / lunch with us / going to / you / aren't

<u>Why aren't you going to eat lunch with us</u>?

5. this way forever / not / we're / live / going to

<u>We're not going to live this way forever</u>.

6. going to / in December / they're / to Colombia / move

<u>They're going to move to Colombia in December</u>.

7. for a new job / when / going to / you / are / look

<u>When are you going to look for a new job</u>?

8. he / take / isn't / the exam with us / going to

<u>He isn't going to take the exam with us</u>.

■ EXERCISE 3   Answer each question using a complete sentence with *be going to*.

Example Are you going to meet your friends tonight?

<u>Yes, I'm going to meet my friends tonight.</u>

1. Where are you going after class?

<u>I'm going to go Home</u>

2. What are you going to do this weekend?

<u>I'm going to do my home work.</u>

3. How are you going to use English in the future?

<u>I'm going to use English for learning Education</u>.

■ EXERCISE 4   Read the paragraph and correct the mistakes. There are 6 mistakes.

Example We ~~is~~ *are* going to the basketball game.

My Community

An article about my community ~~are~~ *is* going to be in the newspaper next week. The story will appear

on the front page. Last week, people in my community made a space for a community garden. The garden *is*

going to have vegetables and flowers. My sister ~~are~~ *is* going to plant the tomatoes. *I'm* going to be responsible

for the watermelons. This garden is going *to* bring people in our community together. The people at the

newspaper wanted to tell about our garden. My mother ~~are~~ *is* going to buy the very first copy of the paper!

Practice 11 *Will* versus *Be going to*

USE	WILL	BE GOING TO
Prediction	My father always exercises and eats well. I think he **will live** a long time.	I think my father **is going to live** a long time.
Fact	The sun **will set** at 6:43 p.m. The population **will increase**.	The sun **is going to set** at 6:43 p.m. The population **is going to increase**.
Scheduled event	The movie **will begin** at 8:00.	The movie **is going to begin** at 8:00.
Plan	–	I **am going to return** to my country in three years.
Promise	I **will** always **love** you.	–
Offer to help	**A:** This box is heavy. **B:** I**'ll carry** it for you	–

■ **EXERCISE 1** Complete the sentence with *will* or *be going to* and the verb in parentheses. In some cases, both answers are possible.

Example (go) Tonight I _____am going to go_____ to a concert.

1. (happen) I have a feeling that something good _will happen/is going to_ ~~happen~~ to me today.

2. (see) The doctor _____will see_____ you as soon as possible.

3. (meet) We _will meet/are going to_ ~~meet~~ in the library to study together.

4. (be) _____Are_____ you _going to be_ there when I get home?

5. (continue) The stock market _will/is go_ probably _continue/going to continue_ to be unpredictable for several more years.

6. (buy) What _are_ ~~are~~ we _going to buy_ him for his birthday?

7. (eat) _____Are_____ n't you _going to eat_ any of this delicious cake?

8. (need) You _will need/are going to_ ~~need~~ an umbrella today.

9. (give) I _will/will give_ you a ride to the shopping mall.

10. (be) You _____will be_____ late if you miss the bus.

11. (graduate) My younger sister _____will graduate_____ from high school next year.

12. (open) Wait! I _____will open_____ the door for you.

13. (go) I _am going to go_ to Brazil this summer.

14. (be) I promise I _____ will be _____ home by midnight.

15. (speak) _____ Are you _____ you _____ going to speak _____ with your teacher after class?

■ **EXERCISE 2**   Complete the sentence using *will* for promises or offers to help. Use *be going to* for plans.

Examples I _____ will _____ never be rude.

I _____ am going to _____ study with Mae tonight.

1. I _____ am going to / will _____ meet my boss at the train station tomorrow.

2. I _____ will _____ mail that letter for you.

3. We _____ are going to _____ move into a larger apartment soon.

4. _____ Will _____ you marry me?

5. I _____ will _____ call you first thing tomorrow.

6. Don't bother stopping at the supermarket. I _____ am going to _____ buy milk on my way home.

■ **EXERCISE 3**   Read the email and correct the mistakes. There are 10 mistakes.

Example I predict that I ~~is~~ *am* going to win first place in the contest.

To: karell@negley*school.com

Subject: Our Class Play

Hi!

Our class play *is going to* be next Tuesday. It *will* start at 7:00 p.m. It *is* ~~are~~ going to be the best play ever! The band *is going to* help us by playing the music. They *are* ~~is~~ going to perform before the play, too. The costumes are very funny. I think they *will* make everyone laugh. You *are* ~~is~~ not going to believe how much fun you will have at the play. I hope you *will* be there next week. I think the seats *are going to* fill up fast! I *will* call you tonight.

Your friend,

Carmen

Will versus *Be going to*   **23**

EXAMPLE	EXPLANATION
Martin Luther King Jr. **lived** in the South. He **organized** peaceful protests.	To make the simple past tense of regular verbs, just add −ed or −d:

	Base Form	Past Forms
	live	*lived*
	organize	*organized*
	carry	*carried*

Dr. King **lived** in the South. He **didn't live** in the North.	Use the past form in affirmative statements. Use *didn't* + the base form of the verb in negative statements.
He **wanted to change** certain laws. He **encouraged** people **to protest** bad laws.	The verb after *to* does not use the past form.

Language Note: We often use *ago* with the simple past:
I lived there 10 years *ago*.

■ EXERCISE 1   Underline the verb. Then rewrite the sentence with the verb in the simple past tense.

Example I <u>will cancel</u> my plane reservation.

<u>I canceled my plane reservation.</u>

1. I travel to Peru with my best friend.

   I traveled to Peru with my best friend

2. The workers are painting the walls of the house.

   The workers are Painted the walls of the house.

3. The secretary cancels all of the doctor's appointments.

   The Secretary Canceled all of the doctor's appointments

4. It rains every day.

   It rained every day.

5. We live in a crowded city.

   We lived in a crowded city

6. You will ask your boss for more money.

   You will aske your boss For more money.

7. My uncle is going to move on Thursday.

   My uncle is moved on thursday.

Problem →

8. The car crashes into the tree.

The car crashed the tree.

9. I will wash the dishes in a couple of hours.

I washed the dishes in a couple of hours.

10. They hope to be the best students in the class.

They hoped to be the best students in the class.

EXERCISE 2 Each simple past tense sentence has 2 underlined words but only 1 mistake. Circle the mistake and write the correct word on the line.

Example She <u>needed</u> to (going) home after the party. _____go_____

1. Yesterday, we <u>needing</u> to <u>go</u> to the store for milk. ___need.___
2. You <u>wanted</u> to (buys) some candy. ___buy___
3. She <u>tried</u> to <u>helped</u> the woman with her groceries. ___try___
4. Alberto <u>asked</u> how to (finding) the vegetables. ___Find___
5. He <u>walked</u> over to (seeing) the tomatoes and corn. ___See___
6. I (cleans) and <u>washed</u> the vegetables from the store. ___cleand___
7. They (likes) to <u>cook</u> vegetables and rice for dinner. ___like___
8. We (stopping) to <u>look</u> at the cakes and donuts. ___stopp___

EXERCISE 3 Read the paragraph and correct the mistakes. There are 7 mistakes.

Example Many people <del>learning</del> folk dances from a variety of countries. _learned_

Quiz-2

Today was cultural day at school. We watch [watched] many types of dances from around the world. Spanish [cultur]

folk dancers performing [performed] in colorful costumes. Mrs. Stamos, my teacher, is from Greece. She promise [promised] to

teach us the Greek chain dance. A young Jamaican dancer lean [Leand] backward and went under a pole during

his limbo dance. A group from Estonia show [showed] us a dance about a spinning wheel. Someone in the audience

request [requested] an Irish square dance. Finally, there was a Mexican dance. A woman dance [danced] around a large hat called

a sombrero. It was a very interesting day!

Practice 13   Simple Past Tense of Irregular Verbs

VERBS WITH NO CHANGE IN PAST				FINAL *D* CHANGES TO *T*	
beat	fit	put	**spit**	bend—**bent**	send—**sent**
bet	hit	quit	**split**	build—**built**	spend—**spent**
cost	hurt	set	**spread**	lend—**lent**	
cut	let	shut			

VERBS WITH VOWEL CHANGES

feel—**felt**	mean—**meant***	dig—**dug**	sting—**stung**
keep—**kept**	sleep—**slept**	hang—**hung**	strike—**struck**
leave—**left**	sweep—**swept**	spin—**spun**	swing—**swung**
lose—**lost**	weep—**wept**	stick—**stuck**	win—**won**
awake—**awoke**	speak—**spoke**	begin—**began**	sing—**sang**
break—**broke**	steal—**stole**	drink—**drank**	sink—**sank**
choose—**chose**	wake—**woke**	forbid—**forbade**	sit—**sat**
freeze—**froze**		ring—**rang**	spring—**sprang**
understand—**understood** stand—**stood**		shrink—**shrank**	swim—**swam**
bring—**brought**	fight—**fought**	blow—**blew**	grow—**grew**
buy—**bought**	teach—**taught**	draw—**drew**	know—**knew**
fall—**fell**	hold—**held**	fly—**flew**	throw—**threw**
arise—**arose**	rise—**rose**	bleed—**bled**	lead—**led**
drive—**drove**	shine—**shone**	feed—**fed**	meet—**met**
ride—**rode**	write—**wrote**	flee—**fled**	read—**read***
sell—**sold**	tell—**told**	find—**found**	wind—**wound**
mistake—**mistook**	take—**took**	lay—**laid**	say—**said****
shake—**shook**		pay—**paid**	
swear—**swore**	wear—**wore**	bite—**bit**	light—**lit**
tear—**tore**		hide—**hid**	slide—**slid**
become—**became**	give—**gave**	run—**ran**	see—**saw**
come—**came**	forgive—**forgave**	forget—**forgot**	shoot—**shot**
eat—**ate**	lie—**lay**	get—**got**	

MISCELLANEOUS CHANGES

be—**was / were**	do—**did**	go—**went**	have—**had**	hear—**heard**	make—**made**

Meant rhymes with *sent.*   **The past form of *read* sounds like *red.*
***Said* rhymes with *bed.*

Language Note: Use the simple past form in affirmative statements. Use *didn't* + the base form of the verb in negative sentences:
She *forgot* to bring the money. I *didn't forget* to bring money.

■ **EXERCISE 1** **Rewrite each sentence using the simple past tense of the irregular verb. Some of the statements are negative.**

Examples The house (shake) in the wind. <u>The house shook in the wind.</u>

The building (not / shake). <u>The building didn't shake.</u>

1. I (not / leave) the house at 7:45 a.m.

_____

2. She (speak) to the class for two hours.

_____

3. He (teach) us how to speak without an accent.

_____

4. We (not / write) in our journals last night.

_____

5. The boys (win) the prize for best spellers.

_____

6. The girls (swim) in the ocean all day.

_____

■ **EXERCISE 2** **Read the conversation and correct the mistakes. There are 7 mistakes.**

Example Edward's sister ~~drive~~ *drove* him to the mall this afternoon.

Kyra: Hurry up! The movie ~~begin~~ *began* five minutes ago.

Marek: I know. The traffic is terrible. It ~~take~~ *took* a long time to get here.

Kyra: That's OK. Hey, is that a new shirt?

Marek: Yes. I ~~buy~~ *bought* it yesterday.

Kyra: It's nice. Where did you ~~putted~~ *put* the tickets?

Marek: I give them to you, right?

Kyra: Oh, no! I take them out of my bag at home.

Practice 14 Negatives and Questions with the Simple Past Tense

WH– WORD	DID / DIDN'T	SUBJECT	VERB	COMPLEMENT	SHORT ANSWER
		My friend	**had**	good grades.	
		She	**didn't have**	bad grades.	
	Did	she	**have**	good grades last year?	Yes, she **did**. /
Where	**did**	she	**go**	to school?	No, she **didn't**.
Why	**didn't**	she	**have**	good grades last year?	

EXAMPLE	EXPLANATION
The student **didn't succeed**. They **weren't** at home yesterday.	Use *didn't* + the base form of the verb in negative statements. Use *wasn't* and *weren't* for *be* in negative statements.
Why did the students **succeed**? **Did** they **take** the same test? **Were** any students unhappy?	Questions use *did* (or sometimes *didn't*) and the base form of the verb. *Be* questions use *was* and *were*.

■ **EXERCISE 1** Ask a question in response to each sentence. Use the time words in parentheses.

Examples He passes the test every week. (last week)

<u>Did he pass the test last week?</u>

He was happy. (not / yesterday)

<u>Wasn't he happy yesterday?</u>

1. The child feels sick today. (yesterday)

   <u>Did they feel sik yesterday?</u>

2. She is dizzy and tired. (yesterday afternoon)

   <u>Does she dizzy and tired yesterday afternoon?</u>

3. She sleeps 10 hours every night. (last night)

   <u>Does she sleep 10 hours last night?</u>

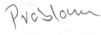 *Problem*

4. The doctors are worried about the child. (not / this past week)

   → <u>Didn't they are worry about the child this past week</u>

5. They find hospital rooms for their patients. (not / this morning)

   _____

6. The child is in bed now. (not / a few minutes ago)

   _____

7. Her father makes her eat some soup. (a few hours ago)

   _____

■ **EXERCISE 2** Answer each question about yourself.

Example Did you go to Paris last year?

<u>No, I didn't go to Paris last year.</u> or <u>Yes, I went to Paris last year.</u>

1. Where did you go yesterday?

   <u>No, I didn't go to yesterday or Yes, I went to College yesterday.</u>

2. How did you get there?

   <u>No, I didn't get there. or Yes I got there.</u>

3. Did you ever fly anywhere?

   <u>No, I didn't fly anywhere. or Yes, I flied anywhere.</u>

4. Whom did you ride with on your trip?

   <u>No, I didn't ride with on my tripe. or yes I ride with on my trip.</u>

5. Were you a student three years ago?

   <u>No, I didn't student three years ago. or Yes, I were a student three years a</u>

6. When did you get this book?

   <u>No, I didn't get this book. or Yes, I got this book.</u>

■ **EXERCISE 3** Read the email and correct the mistakes. There are 7 mistakes.

Example Did you clean your room today? No, I ~~did~~. ^{didn't}

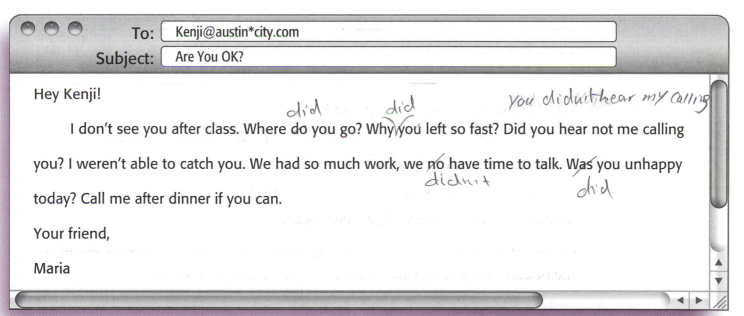

To: Kenji@austin*city.com

Subject: Are You OK?

Hey Kenji!

   I don't see you after class. Where do you go? Why you left so fast? Did you hear not me calling

you? I weren't able to catch you. We had so much work, we no have time to talk. Was you unhappy

today? Call me after dinner if you can.

Your friend,

Maria

EXAMPLE	EXPLANATION
Greta loves music. Yesterday, **she** bought five new CDs.	We use subject pronouns to take the place of subject nouns.
She also bought a CD player. She bought **it** downtown.	We use object pronouns to take the place of object nouns.
She got some CDs for her boyfriend. She got the CDs for **him**.	An object pronoun can follow a preposition.

Language Notes:
1. We use pronouns to take the place of nouns.
2. The object pronouns are *me, you, him, her, it, us,* and *them*. Compare subject and object pronouns:

Subject Pronouns	Object Pronouns	Examples: S	V	O
I	*me*	*You*	*see*	*me.*
you	*you*	*I*	*see*	*you.*
he	*him*	*She*	*sees*	*him.*
she	*her*	*He*	*sees*	*her.*
it	*it*	*I*	*see*	*it.*
we	*us*	*They*	*see*	*us.*
they	*them*	*We*	*see*	*them.*

■ **EXERCISE 1** Write the subject or object pronoun to complete each sentence.

Example What are flea markets? __They__ are places where you can buy things secondhand.

People who go to flea markets are looking for bargains. They often find
(1) _____them_____. My aunt met her husband at a flea market. He sold
(2) _____her_____ some secondhand jewelry. (3) _____it_____
wasn't very expensive. Then he asked (4) _____her_____ to have a cup of
tea with (5) _____him_____. Now he teases (6) _____her_____ by
saying that she was the best bargain (7) _____he_____ ever found.
She tells (8) _____him_____ that he should have looked for a better deal.

■ **EXERCISE 2** Unscramble the words to make a correct sentence.

Example English / I / you / helped / learn

I helped you learn English.

1. to me / she / on the phone / talked

   She talked to me on the Phone.

2. we / ice cream / them / bought

   We bought ice cream

3. loves / she / him / very much

She loves him very much

4. want / him / to / I / to talk

I want to talk to him.

5. he / a stereo / wants / for us / to buy

He wants to buy a stereo for us.

6. them / I / don't / know / very well

I don't know them very well.

7. to listen / he / her / wants

He wants her to listen.

8. I / like / tennis / play / to / her / with

I like to play tennis with her.

9. yesterday / the present / gave / him / she

She gave him the present, yesterday. Yesterday she gave him the present.

10. asked / we / about it / her

We asked about it her.

■ EXERCISE 3 Write a sentence using each pair of pronouns.

Example (them / you) <u>You gave them a beautiful gift.</u>

1. (she / me) _She gave me a book._

2. (him / I) _I love with him for ever._

3. (us / they) _They helpe us from along time._

4. (we / you) _We gave you a Pain_

■ EXERCISE 4 Read the paragraph and correct the mistakes. There are 7 mistakes.

Example My friends and ~~me~~ like to spend time outdoors.

---

www.blog*diary.com/Marissa

June 25: Luiz and me asked his mother to drive I to a nearby state park. He and me went there today. At first, us walked on a marked trail through the woods. Before long, us were in a snowy area far from the trail. At noon, Luiz and me followed our tracks back to the path. Him and I had the best time of our lives!

NOUN	ENDING	EXAMPLE
Singular noun: cat	Add apostrophe + s.	I put food in the **cat's** dish.
Plural noun ending in –s: boys	Add apostrophe only.	Open the windows in the **boys'** room.
Irregular plural noun: children	Add apostrophe + s.	Open the windows in the **children's** room.
Names that end in –s: Charles	Add apostrophe only. or Add apostrophe + s.	This is **Charles'** cousin. This is **Charles's** cousin.

Language Notes: 1. We use the possessive form for people and other living things:
I borrowed my *sister's* car. *Julia's* friend is from Armenia.
2. For inanimate objects, we usually use "the _____ of _____":
We usually use the door at *the back of the house*.
3. We can use possessive adjectives to show possession. The possessive adjectives are
my, your, his, her, its, our, and *their*:
I'm wearing *my* coat. That's *your* bag
4. We can use a possessive adjective and a possessive noun together:
Could you give me *your boss's* phone number?

■ **EXERCISE 1**   Fill in each blank with the correct possessive form.

Example My wife _'s___ cooking is even better than my mother _'s___ cooking.

1. Stop! That's James _____ toothbrush.
2. Can you get me Ms. Reese _____ email address?
3. Football players _____ uniforms are very hard to get clean.
4. Your company _____ new Web site is really well designed.
5. Other companies _____ Web sites aren't nearly so attractive.
6. You'll find the dresses you want in the girls _____ department.
7. You should go to the children _____ shoe department.
8. Women _____ clothing is on the fourth floor.
9. Go to the third floor for men _____ clothing.
10. Don't pull the cat _____ tail!
11. She's wearing her grandmother _____ bracelet.
12. Everyone wants to go to John _____ party Saturday night.
13. Quick, hide the cake! I hear Daddy _____ footsteps!
14. Let me take a look at my boss _____ schedule.

EXERCISE 2 Use the words to write a sentence that contains a possessive form. (The words are not in the correct order.)

Example the table / the leg / is broken

<u>The leg of the table is broken.</u>

1. where is / wallet / Papa

   _____

2. he is wearing / shirt / Dmitri

   _____

3. someone tore / the book / cover

   _____

4. the chair / the arm / is broken

   _____

5. what is / this car / the price

   _____

6. cap / missing / the pen

   _____

EXERCISE 3 Read the email and correct the mistakes. There are 7 mistakes.

Example That is ~~somebody~~ lost puppy. *somebody's*

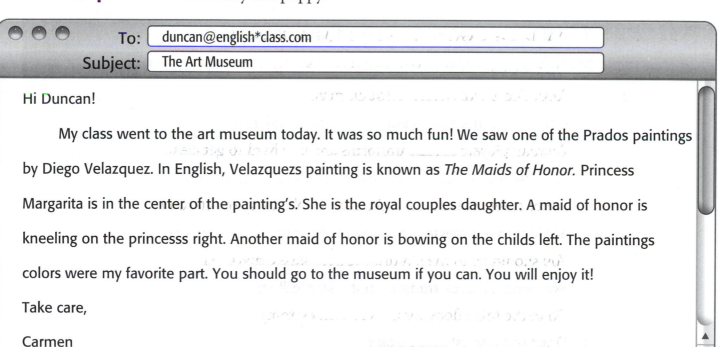

To: duncan@english*class.com

Subject: The Art Museum

Hi Duncan!

My class went to the art museum today. It was so much fun! We saw one of the Prados paintings

by Diego Velazquez. In English, Velazquezs painting is known as *The Maids of Honor.* Princess

Margarita is in the center of the painting's. She is the royal couples daughter. A maid of honor is

kneeling on the princesss right. Another maid of honor is bowing on the childs left. The paintings

colors were my favorite part. You should go to the museum if you can. You will enjoy it!

Take care,

Carmen

WHOSE + NOUN	AUXILIARY VERB	SUBJECT	VERB	ANSWER
Whose dress	**did**	she	**borrow?**	She borrowed *Rika's* dress.
Whose pen	**can**	I	**use?**	You can use *my* pen.
Whose sister	**is**	that?		That is *his* sister.

Language Notes: 1. *Whose* + a noun asks a question about possession.
2. *Whose* shows possession; *who's* is the contraction for *who is* or *who has*.

■ **EXERCISE 1**   Write a follow-up question with *whose* for each statement.

Example I found someone's books in the library.

<u>Whose books did you find in the library?</u>

1. Someone's book was left in the back seat of the car.

   Whose book was in the back seat of the car

2. I want to try someone's dessert recipe.

   Whose dessert recipe do you want to trey.

3. She should take my advice.

   Whose advice should she take?

4. The teacher corrected someone's homework.

   Whose home work did the teacher correcte?

5. They went to their friends' house.

   Whose house did they go to?

6. The robbers used someone's key to enter the house.

   Problem   Whose key the robbers did use to enter the house?

7. The police discovered someone's jewelry in a paper bag.

   Whose jewelry did the Police discovere in a Paper bag.

8. Someone's composition will win the award.

   Whoes Composition will win the a ward?

9. Someone's dog is wandering around in the street.

   Whoes dog is wandering around in the street

10. It's chasing someone's cat.

    Whow cat is it chasing?

11. The cat is climbing someone's tree.

    Whow tree is the climbing?

EXERCISE 2   Write questions about the nouns in each sentence. Begin each question with *Whose*.

Example What a beautiful car.

Quiz-2

Whose car is it?

1. That's not your umbrella.

   Whose umbrella is that?

2. You got an invitation to a party.

   Whose party did you get an invitation?

3. I don't recognize this coat.

   Whose coat is this?

4. This isn't my medicine in the medicine cabinet.

   Whose this medicine in the medicine cabinet?

5. Look at this mess!

   Whose mess is this?

6. I found this camera.

   Whose camera did you find?

EXERCISE 3   Read the conversation and correct the mistakes. There are 6 mistakes.

Example ~~Who's~~ *Whose* car is this?

Rosa: ~~Whose~~ *Who's* going to the beach with us on Saturday?

Jenny: I'm not sure. I think Nate and Amro want to go, but they don't have a car.
~~Who's~~ *Whose* car can we go in?

Rosa: Bob has a car.

Jenny: ~~Whose~~ *Who's* Bob?

Rosa: He's Nate's brother.

Jenny: Oh, OK. We need to bring a cooler. ~~Who's~~ *Whose* cooler can we bring?

Rosa: We can bring mine.

Jenny: OK. ~~Whose~~ *Who's* got a CD player? We like to listen to music at the beach.

Rosa: Amro has one, I think.

Jenny: Great. ~~Who's~~ *whose* house should we meet at?

Rosa: Let's meet at your house at 10:00.

Jenny: Great! See you then!

Practice 18 Possessive Adjectives and Pronouns

EXAMPLE	EXPLANATION
That is **my** book. **Our** apartment is small.	The possessive adjective must come before a noun. We can't use it alone or without a noun.
That book is **mine**. (mine = my book) That apartment is **ours**. (ours = our apartment)	The possessive pronoun takes the place of a noun. It never comes before a noun.

Language Notes: 1. Be careful with *his* and *her*:

I have a married *brother*. *His* wife is very nice.

The *bride* looks beautiful. *Her* father looks proud.
2. When we use a possessive pronoun, we omit the noun.
   Her dress is white. ⟶ *Yours* is blue.
3. Compare subject pronouns, possessive adjectives, and possessive pronouns:

SUBJECT PRONOUN	POSSESSIVE ADJECTIVE	POSSESSIVE PRONOUN
I	my	mine
you	your	yours
he	his	his
she	her	hers
it	its	–
we	our	ours
they	their	theirs

■ **EXERCISE 1** For each underlined pair of adjectives or pronouns, ⌾circle the correct possessive form.

Example Put your / yours coat on. It's cold outside!

1. This bag is not mine. I think it's your / yours.
2. She is a doctor. Her / Hers sister is a lawyer.
3. Is this mine or your / yours?
4. That's his office. It's not my / mine.
5. I don't know their / theirs address.
6. I think that house is their / theirs.
7. This table is our / ours.
8. Your / Yours MP3 player is broken. Why don't you borrow my / mine?
9. Our / Ours car is white. They / Theirs is red.
10. Her / Hers hair is the same length as my / mine.
11. Do you want me to take yours / your picture?
12. His mother is from my / mine country.

13. Please don't take my / mine textbook without my / mine permission.
14. Their / Theirs children are coming over with their / theirs friends.
15. This isn't her / hers scarf. Her / Hers is blue.
16. Our / Ours vacation was as good as your / yours.

■ **EXERCISE 2** **Rewrite each sentence. Replace the underlined portion with the correct possessive pronoun or possessive adjective.**

Example This is a picture of <u>John and Anne's</u> new baby.

<u>This is a picture of their new baby.</u>

1. <u>The boys'</u> clothes are in the washing machine.

Their clothes are in the washing machine.

2. That suitcase isn't <u>your suitcase.</u>

That suitcase isn't yours.

3. <u>The little girl's</u> kitten ran away.

Her kitten ran away.

4. The next day, the kitten returned to <u>the little girl's</u> family's house.

The next day, the kitten returned to her family house

5. My pen ran out of ink, so I'm going to use <u>your pen</u>.

My pen ran out of ink, so I'm going to use yours.

6. She announced that <u>Jim's</u> flight would arrive early.

She announced that his flight would arrive early

7. <u>Jeanne's</u> flight arrived earlier than <u>our flight.</u>

his flight arrived earlier than ours.

■ **EXERCISE 3** **Read the conversation and correct the mistakes. There are 9 mistakes.**

Example That is ~~mine~~ **my** shirt. Where is ~~your~~ **yours**?

Tanya: Have you seen ~~mine~~ **my** dog?

Lilly: No, I haven't seen yours dog.

Tanya: This is hers collar. I found it in ours yard.

Lilly: How do you think she lost it **her** collar?

Tanya: She likes to rub hers neck on the ground.

Lilly: ~~Mine~~ **My** dog was lost last week. I was sad.

Tanya: What is hers name? Did you find her?

Lilly: Yes, I was so happy. Let's look for yours dog now.

WH– WORD	DO / DOES / DID	SUBJECT	VERB	COMPLEMENT
What	**does**	The bride she She **Who**	**throws** **throw**? **throws** **catches**	something. the bouquet. it?
What	**did**	The guests they Some guests **How many** guests	**brought** **bring**? **brought** **brought**	something. gifts. gifts?
Why	**do**	Some women they **Which** women	**try** **try** **try**	to catch the bouquet. to catch it? to catch it?
		Something **What**	**happened** **happened**	next. next?

Language Notes: 1. Questions about the subject are different from other questions. They don't include *do*, *does*, or *did*.
2. We usually answer a subject question with a subject and an auxiliary verb:
   Who caught the bouquet?   The bride's cousin *did*.
3. *What happened* is a subject question. We usually answer with a different verb:
   What happened after the wedding?   The bride and groom *went* on their honeymoon.
4. After *who*, use the *–s* form for the simple present tense. After *how many*, use the base form of the verb. After other questions, use the *–s* form or the base form of the verb, depending on whether the noun is singular or plural:
   Who has the prettiest dress?   *Which girl was* the bridesmaid?
   How many people *want* to dance?   *Which girls were* the nicest?

■ **EXERCISE 1**   **Write a question about the subject of each sentence.**

Example Who sent you the information by email?

   Answer: My brother sent me the information by email.

1. _Whoa wrote the answerson?_

   Answer: Tommy wrote the answers on the palm of his hand.

2. _Who Caught the robbers ?_

   Answer: Two police officers caught the robbers.

3. _How usually brings his sister?_

   Answer: Jorge usually brings his sister.

4. _How always carry first-aid equipment?_

   Answer: The climbers always carry first-aid equipment.

5. _How took every one to dinner?_

   Answer: <u>Chang</u> took everyone to dinner.

6. _What destroyed several villages?_

   Answer: <u>The earthquake</u> destroyed several villages.

7. _Whose ship survived the tsunami?_

   Answer: <u>Our</u> ship survived the tsunami.

8. _Who are your grandparents a coming to see?_

   Answer: My grandparents are coming to see <u>us</u>.

9. _____

   Answer: <u>Five</u> firefighters fought the fire.

■ EXERCISE 2 (Circle) the letter of the best response for each question.

Example Who met her at the train station?

   (**a.** Her father did.)   **b.** Her father did meet.

1. What broke the window?

   (**a.**) A baseball did.   **b.** A baseball did break.

2. Who ate my strawberries?

   a. I do.   (**b.**) I did.

3. What caused the accident?

   (**a.**) A speeding driver did.   **b.** A speeding driver did cause the accident.

4. Who told you?

   a. She.   (**b.**) She did.

■ EXERCISE 3 Read the conversation and correct the mistakes. There are 8 mistakes.

Example Something ~~happens~~ _happened_ after class.

Phil: How many people come to Laura's piano concert?

Sara: About 20 people came~~s~~. It was great.

Phil: Did Juan and Olivia ~~came~~ _come_?

Sara: No, they ~~not~~ _didn't_.

Phil: Really? Why _didn't_ they ~~no~~ come?

Sara: I don't know. But we have a great time after the concert.

Phil: Oh? What happen_ed_ after the concert?

Sara: We ~~take~~ _took_ Laura out to dinner at the new Italian restaurant.

SUBJECT	VERB	REFLEXIVE PRONOUN
I	see	**myself**.
You (singular)	see	**yourself**.
He	sees	**himself**.
She	sees	**herself**.
It	sees	**itself**.
We	see	**ourselves**.
You (plural)	see	**yourselves**.
They	see	**themselves**.

EXAMPLE	EXPLANATION
Sylvia sometimes blames **herself**. (DO) I tell **myself** that he loves me. (IO) Be good to **yourself**. (OP)	A reflexive pronoun can be a direct object (DO), an indirect object (IO), or the object of a preposition (OP).
She hates to eat **by herself**. She has to do everything **all by herself**.	We often add *all by* before the reflexive pronoun to mean *alone*.

Language Notes: 1. If the subject and object are the same, we use a reflexive pronoun as the object.
2. After an imperative, use *yourself* or *yourselves*, depending on whether *you* refers to one person or more:
Get *yourself* a lawyer. (1 person)
Get *yourselves* a lawyer. (more than 1 person)

■ **EXERCISE 1**   **Write the correct reflexive pronoun in the blank.**

Example She gave _____herself_____ a party.

1. We sang __ourselves__ a song.

2. The old man drew __himself__ a map.

3. The bird saw __itself__ in the mirror.

4. He is in love with __himself__.

5. It's so loud. I can't hear __myself__ think.

6. If you're hungry, make __yourself / yourselves__ a sandwich.

7. We gave __ourselves__ a pat on the back.

8. He gave __himself__ a headache worrying about the situation.

9. Don't drive __himself__ crazy trying to solve this problem.

10. Can you teach __yourself__ vocabulary?

11. If the alarm doesn't work, you'll have to wake __yourself__ up.

12. I go home every night and cook __myself__ dinner.

13. They can't earn enough money to support ___themselves___.

14. Look! That man over there is talking to ___himself___.

15. She ate the whole cake, and she made ___herself___ sick.

16. Babies can't feed ___themselves___.

17. We saved our money until we had enough to buy ___ourselves___ a house.

18. Dennis hurt ___himself___ with the electric drill.

■ EXERCISE 2   Circle the correct reflexive pronoun.

Example His problem is that he doesn't have any confidence in (himself)/ herself.

1. You have to turn the key in the ignition. The car won't start (itself)/ yourself.

2. She didn't know anyone in the class, so she introduced themselves / (herself) to the student next to her.

3. For three months, the students prepared themself / (themselves) for the exam.

4. The older sister told her younger sister ghost stories until she even frightened (herself)/ themselves.

5. Don't let that little boy play with that knife. He'll cut (himself)/ themselves.

6. No one invited us to the party, so we invited ourself / (ourselves).

■ EXERCISE 3   Read the paragraph and correct the mistakes. There are 7 mistakes.

Example Did Ms. Chan make the announcement ~~herselves~~ ? *herself*

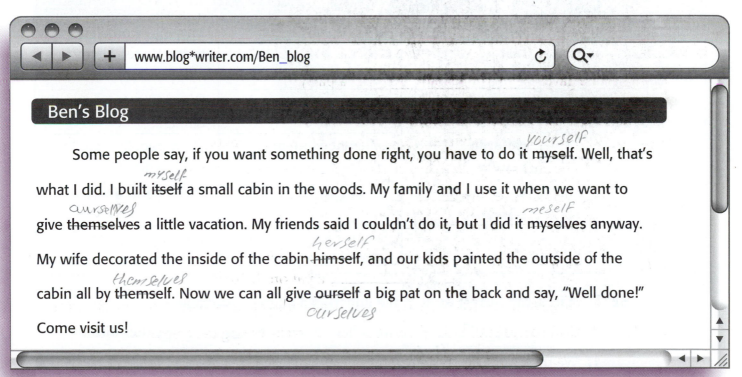

Ben's Blog

Some people say, if you want something done right, you have to do it ~~myself~~. *yourself* Well, that's what I did. I built ~~itself~~ a small cabin in the woods. *myself* My family and I use it when we want to give ~~themselves~~ a little vacation. *ourselves* My friends said I couldn't do it, but I did it ~~myselves~~ anyway. *meself*

My wife decorated the inside of the cabin ~~himself~~, and our kids painted the outside of the *herself* cabin all by ~~themself~~. Now we can all give ~~ourself~~ a big pat on the back and say, "Well done!" *themselves* *ourselves*

Come visit us!

Practice 21 Noun Plurals

REGULAR NOUN PLURALS

WORD ENDINGS	SINGULAR	PLURAL ADDITION	PLURAL
Vowel	bee, banana	+ s	bees, bananas
s, ss, sh, ch, x, z	dish, watch	+ es	dishes, watches
Voiceless consonant	cat, lip	+ s	cats, lips
Voiced consonant	card, pin	+ s	cards, pins
Vowel + y	boy, day	+ s	boys, days
Consonant + y	lady, story	y + ies	ladies, stories
Vowel + o	video, radio	+ s	videos, radios
Consonant + o *Exceptions: photos, pianos, solos, altos, sopranos, autos, avocados	potato, hero	+ es*	potatoes, heroes
f or fe **Exceptions: beliefs, chiefs, roofs, cliffs, chefs, sheriffs	leaf, knife	f + ves**	leaves, knives

IRREGULAR NOUN PLURALS

SINGULAR	PLURAL	EXPLANATION	EXAMPLE
woman foot goose	women feet geese	Vowel change	Men and women came to the United States from many countries.
sheep fish	sheep fish	No change	He caught six fish for dinner.
child person	children people	Different word form	Many people came to the celebration.
	pajamas, pants, scissors	No singular form	Those pants are clean.
news, politics	–	Singular form ends in –s; no plural form	The news from my doctor is good.

■ **EXERCISE 1** (Circle) the correct form of the <u>underlined</u> noun or pronoun.

Example When I was a (kid) / kids, we always had to wash the dish / (dishes) after dinner.

1. We took a couple of (sandwiches) / sandwichs with us for lunch.
2. Dress the baby in his pajama / pajamas and put him to bed.
3. A few basketball players are 7 feet / foot tall.

4. Most of the news <u>seems</u> / seem bad.

5. During the rain, all of the seates / <u>seats</u> / seat in the stadium got wet.

6. I washed my jeans, and it / <u>they</u> shrank so much that I can't wear it / <u>them</u>.

7. Could you get me two <u>boxes</u> / boxs of crackers from the cabinet?

8. You should wash your <u>glasses</u> / glasss. They're so dirty you can't see anything.

9. Let's get a couple of new <u>suitcases</u> / suitcase for our trip.

10. We'll remember our wedding day for the rest of our <u>lives</u> / lifes.

11. This paper is going to take me at least three more <u>hours</u> / houres to write.

12. There is a monument to the <u>heroes</u> / heros of the revolution.

■ **EXERCISE 2**   **Write the plural form of each noun.**

Example pin _____pins_____

1. month ___months___
2. child ___children___
3. fruit ___fruits/fruit___
4. tooth ___teeth___
5. mouse ___mices___
6. cake ___cakes___
7. mosquito ___mosquitoes___
   ___mosquitos___

8. potato ___potatoes___
9. tree ___treees___
10. boy ___boys___
11. fire ___fires___
12. fly ___flies___
13. knife ___knives___
14. piece ___pieces___

■ **EXERCISE 3**   **Read the email and correct the mistakes. There are 7 mistakes.**

Example Those ~~woman~~ ^{women} visited the pumpkin farm.

To: sondra@school*hall.com

Subject: Our New Town!

Hi Sondra!

We have finally moved into our new house in Fairview. Tax are high here, but our neighborhood^s park are excellent. We are only a five-minute drive from two different beach. Houses with ~~patio~~ are common on our street. A machine with three huge brush keeps the streets clean. From a hill near our house, you can see several valley. On our walks in the hills, we occasionally see wild turkey. I really think I will like living here!

Magaly

(handwritten annotations: houses, taxes, parks, beaches, patios, brushesh, valleys, hills, severals, hill, turkeys)

Practice 22 Using the Singular and Plural for Generalizations

EXAMPLE	EXPLANATION
A child needs love.	To make a generalization, we use a singular noun after
Children need love.	*a* or *an* or the plural noun with no article. When we make
A big city has a lot of traffic.	a generalization, we say that something is true of the noun
Big cities have a lot of traffic.	in general.

Language Notes: 1. We use the singular form of *hundred, million,* etc. to talk about an exact number:
I invited *a hundred* people to my wedding.
2. We use the plural form of *hundreds, millions,* etc. to talk about an inexact number:
Hundreds of people attended the basketball game.
3. After *every* and *each,* we use a singular noun. After *all,* we use a plural noun.

■ EXERCISE 1   Decide if the expression is *specific* or *general*. Write your decision on the line.

Examples children _____general_____   the child _____specific_____

1. the geese ___specific___   7. hundreds of cooks ___G___
2. ten geese ___specific___   8. all working people ___G___
3. a goose ___G___   9. an emotion ___G___
4. every mother ___S___   10. the emotion ___S___
5. each person ___S___   11. emotions ___G___
6. one thousand drivers ___S___ 12. two emotions ___S___

■ EXERCISE 2   Read the sentence. Decide if it is a generalization or a specific statement. (Circle) the best answer.

Example (A vegetarian) / The vegetarian is someone who doesn't eat meat.

1. A vegetarian / (The vegetarian) refused to eat the chicken we offered her.
2. I love (children) / the children.
3. (The children) / Children in my neighborhood are very friendly.
4. Every (child) / children should learn a second language.
5. All of the person / (people) voted for her.
6. She spent about (two hundred dollars) / hundreds of dollars on that table.
7. Women / The women are more expressive than (men) / the men.
8. Life / The life can be difficult.
9. Life / (The life) of a fruit fly is short.
10. There are exactly (four thousand) / thousands of seats in the auditorium.
11. (History) / The history is an interesting subject.
12. I like to study history / (the history) of my country.

13. Did you ask all of the <u>student</u> / ⟨students⟩ to come to the play?

14. You should eat ⟨vegetables⟩ / <u>the vegetables</u> every day.

■ **EXERCISE 3** **Write a sentence with the word as the subject. Make the sentence either specific or general.**

Examples teachers (general) <u>*Teachers want the best for their students.*</u>

teachers (specific) <u>*The teachers at my school don't work at night.*</u>

1. politician (specific)

_____

2. politician (general)

_____

3. hundreds of people (general)

_____

4. one hundred people (specific)

_____

■ **EXERCISE 4** **Read the email and correct the mistakes. There are 8 mistakes.**

Example We saw ~~the~~ *a* hundred birds in the sky.

To:	dsalvatore@mail*2*u.com
Subject:	Hope You're Feeling Better!

Dear Uncle David,

My mom told me that you have ~~the~~ *a* bad cold. That's terrible!

I got you some books at *the* library. If you want, I can bring them to your house this afternoon. I got

you some books about the history of airplanes and three books about gardening. I know you like *the* a

gardening books.

Do you remember when I was sick last year? I had *a* bad cold, too. I think it was in October. I had

to stay home from school for *a* whole week!

I'll come to your house after school. I have ~~the~~ *a* cell phone now, too. You can call me at 555-2201

if you want me to bring you anything else.

Take care,

Ben

These are some ways to distinguish count and noncount nouns:

GROUP A: Nouns that have no distinct, separate parts. We look at the whole.

milk	wine	poultry	meat	thunder	electricity
oil	yogurt	soup	butter	cholesterol	lightning
water	pork	bread	paper	blood	air

GROUP B: Nouns that have parts that are too small or insignificant to count.

rice	salt	hair	grass	sand
sugar	popcorn	snow	corn	

GROUP C: Nouns that are categories of things. The members of the category are not the same.

money or **cash** (nickels, dimes, dollars)   **fruit** (cherries, apples, grapes)
food (vegetables, meat, spaghetti)   **makeup** (lipstick, rouge, mascara)
furniture (chairs, tables, beds)   **homework** (compositions, exercises)
clothing (sweaters, pants, dresses)   **jewelry** (necklaces, bracelets, rings)
mail (letters, packages, postcards, fliers)

GROUP D: Nouns that are abstractions.

love	happiness	nutrition	music	information
life	education	intelligence	art	nature
time	experience	unemployment	work	help
truth	crime	pollution	health	noise
beauty	advice	patience	trouble	energy
luck	knowledge	poverty	fun	friendship

GROUP E: Subjects of study.

history	grammar	biology	physical education
chemistry	geometry	math / mathematics	music
English	Spanish	political science	art

Language Note: Some nouns can be used as count nouns in some sentences and as noncount nouns in other sentences depending on the meaning:
I washed my *hair*. I found a *hair* in my soup.

■ **EXERCISE 1**   These are some things that people can buy at a grocery store. Write *count* or *noncount* next to each word.

Example rice _____noncount_____

1. candy ___noncount___
2. onion ___count___
3. bread ___noncount___
4. oil ___noncount___
5. flour ___noncount___
6. pickle ___count___

7. soy sauce _non Count_   9. toothbrush _Count_

8. toothpaste _non Count_   10. sugar _non Count_

■ EXERCISE 2   Circle the best form of the underlined word.

Example Too much (coffee)/ coffees makes a person nervous.

> People who want to stay healthy and slim should watch what they eat. Food with a lot of (1) butter / butters can make a person obese and can harm the heart. (2) Sugar / Sugars makes a person gain weight too. Eating a lot of (3) rice / rices, (4) noodle / noodles, or (5) bread / breads can make a person gain weight as well.
>
> People with (6) food / foods allergies must also be careful of what they eat. Some people can't eat (7) wheat / wheats, so they can't eat (8) bread / breads or (9) noodle / noodles that are made from wheat. Others are allergic to milk (10) product / products, so they can't drink milk or eat (11) cheese / cheeses or (12) ice cream / ice creams. If a person is very allergic to a (13) food / foods, eating it can endanger his or her (14) life / lives. (15) Knowledges / Knowledge about food can save your life.

■ EXERCISE 3   Read the email and correct the mistakes. There are 9 mistakes.

Example ~~Paper~~ The paper was faded because it was in ^the sun.

To: carmen.read@mather*s*k.com

Subject: My Band

Hey Carmen!

Guess what . . . I'm starting my own bands! There are three peoples in the band. They are all in

my histories class at school. We usually practice at nights. Last night, we gave a concert for some of our

neighbors. We served popcorns and juice, and everybody had a great times. Unfortunately, the noises

was too much for my cat. She is hiding in our basement. I put some foods in her bowl, but she won't

come out!

I'll see you at schools!

Becca

Practice 24   Quantities with Noncount Nouns

BY CONTAINER	BY PORTION	BY MEASUREMENT
a **bottle** of water	a **slice / piece** of bread	an **ounce** of sugar
a **carton** of milk	a **piece** of meat	a **quart** of oil
a **jar** of pickles	a **piece** of cake	a **pound** of meat
a **can** of soda	a **strip** of bacon	a **gallon** of milk
a **cup** of yogurt	a **bowl** of soup	a **pint** of ice cream
a **glass** of water	a **piece / sheet** of paper	
a **bag** of flour	a **slice** of pizza	
a **box** of paper clips	a **scoop** of ice cream	
	a **stick** of butter	

BY SHAPE / WHOLE PIECE		OTHER
a **loaf** of bread	a **roll** of film	a **piece** of mail
an **ear** of corn	a **bar / piece** of candy	a **piece** of furniture
a **piece** of fruit	a **tube** of toothpaste	a **piece** of advice
a **head** of lettuce	a **bar** of soap	a **piece** of information
		a **work** of art
		a homework **assignment**

■ **EXERCISE 1**   Rewrite the phrase using the correct quantity.

Example a jar of cake _a piece of cake_

1. a bottle of cereal _a bowl of cereal_
2. a jar of soap _a bar of soap_
3. a bag of jam _a jar of jam_
4. a box of milk _a carton of milk_
5. a can of butter _a stick of butter_
6. a bar of sugar _a cup of sugar_
7. a stick of flour _a bag of flour_
8. a loaf of chocolate _a bar of chocolate_
9. a teaspoon of candy _a piece of candy_
10. a carton of beans _a can of beans_

■ **EXERCISE 2**   Read the conversation between Monica and Stephen as they plan their shopping trip. Use words from the box to fill in the blanks.

Example I need to buy two heads of _____ lettuce _____ for the salad.

cereal	beans	flour	margarine	toothpaste
mayonnaise	gas	bread	meat	milk	~~lettuce~~

Monica: Let's go shopping for groceries. If you check the pantry, I'll make a list.

Stephen: OK. Let's see. We need (1) a can of _beans_,
(2) a box of _cereal_, (3) a quart of
milk, and (4) a pound of _meat_.

Monica:	Anything else?
Stephen:	Yes, I need (5) a bag of _____ flour _____ and (6) a stick of _____ margarine _____ for the cake I want to make tonight.
Monica:	Good. I need (7) a tube of _____ toothpaste _____. How about you? Do you need anything else?
Stephen:	Maybe (8) a loaf of _____ chocolate _____ and (9) a jar of _____ candy _____ for sandwiches. I think that's all.
Monica:	Great. Let's go to the store.
Stephen:	Oh, don't let me forget that we also need to put (10) a few gallons of _____ beans _____ in the car.

■ **EXERCISE 3** **Think about the items in your kitchen at home. List them with quantity expressions.**

Examples a can of tomatoes

a bag of oranges

In my kitchen at home, I have:

1. _____

2. _____

3. _____

■ **EXERCISE 4** **Read the email and correct the mistakes. There are 6 mistakes.**

Example Audra drank a ~~slice~~ cup of milk.

To: emma@english*school.com

Subject: Our Picnic

Hi Emma,

How are you? I'm sorry that you couldn't come to our picnic on Saturday. It was lots of fun. My

Slices/Pieces

sister ate three cartons of watermelon. Her fingers were really sticky! We had lots of food at the picnic.

Carton/Gallon   *bags*   *loaf*   *Pounds*

There was a slice of juice, several glasses of chips, a pound of bread, two bowls of meat, and three

boxes/bags/Packages

pints of cookies. I liked the apple pie the best. I had two pieces! I can't wait for the next picnic. I hope

you can make it next time!

Love,

Jenn

There + a Form of Be

	THERE	BE	ARTICLE / QUANTITY	NOUN	PLACE OR TIME
Count	**There**	**will be**	a	game	at 2:00 p.m. tomorrow.
	There	**are**	two	sandwiches	in the refrigerator.
Noncount	**There**	**was**	some	good news	on the front page.
	There	**is**	no	water	on the moon.

Language Note: Observe the word order in questions with *there*:
Is there life on Mars? No, there probably isn't.
Are there any more messages for me? Yes, there are.
How many messages *are there?* There are four.

■ **EXERCISE 1** Write *There is* or *There are* before each article or quantity + noun.

Example _____There is_____ a large school next to my apartment.

1. ____There is____ a great selection of shoes at the mall.
2. ____There is____ delicious popcorn at the movie theater.
3. ____There is____ no homework tonight.
4. ____There is____ a red sports car in the parking lot.
5. ____There are____ some vegetables and noodles in my soup.
6. ____There are____ two computers for sale.
7. ____There is____ some lemonade on the table.
8. ____There are____ many happy students in this class.

■ **EXERCISE 2** Write *Is there, Are there, Was there,* or *Were there* to complete the question.

Example _____Was there_____ a party last night?

1. ____Were there____ any students in the library yesterday?
2. ____Are there____ any good movies out right now?
3. ____Were there____ any children in the park an hour ago?
4. ____Is there____ anything for dinner tonight?
5. ____Was there____ enough time for yesterday's test?
6. __Are there / were there__ any phone messages today?
7. ____Were there____ any emails yesterday afternoon?

■ **EXERCISE 3** Fill in the blank with a word from the box. Use each noun only once.

Example Is there any _____meat_____ on my sandwich?

furniture	information	election	children	picture
~~meat~~	credit cards	onions	schedule	

1. Are there any _____ onions _____ on my sandwich?

2. How many homeless _____ children _____ are there in this city?

3. There's some good _____ information _____ on the bulletin board.

4. There's an _____ election _____ every four years.

5. There are two _____ credit cards _____ in my wallet.

6. There's a _____ picture _____ of my family in my wallet.

7. There's a _____ schedule _____ of today's movies in the newspaper.

8. Is there any _____ furniture _____ in the apartment?

■ EXERCISE 4 Unscramble the words to make a sentence with *there*.

Example the swimming pool / are / two girls / in / there

<u>There are two girls in the swimming pool.</u>

1. is / on my desk / there / a lamp

   <u>There is a lamp on my desk.</u>

2. there / many ducks / were / on the pond

   <u>There were many ducks on the pond.</u>

3. was / at the college / a great professor / there

   <u>There was a great professor at the college.</u>

4. this morning / was / about the weather / there / bad news

   <u>There was bad news about the weather this morning.</u>

■ EXERCISE 5 Read the paragraph and correct the mistakes. There are 6 mistakes.

Example There ~~are~~ *is* a radio in my car.

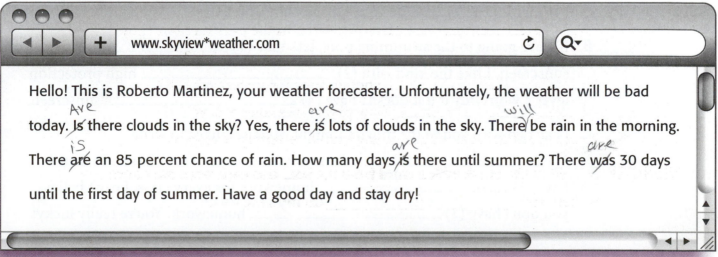

Hello! This is Roberto Martinez, your weather forecaster. Unfortunately, the weather will be bad
today. *Are* Is there clouds in the sky? Yes, there *are* is lots of clouds in the sky. There *will* be rain in the morning.
There *is* are an 85 percent chance of rain. How many days *are* is there until summer? There *are* was 30 days
until the first day of summer. Have a good day and stay dry!

Practice 26 Some, Any, A, No, A little, A few, and Several

	SINGULAR COUNT	PLURAL COUNT	NONCOUNT
Affirmative	There's **a** clock in the kitchen.	There are (**some**) windows in the kitchen. I have (**a few**) questions. I have (**several**) mistakes on my composition.	There's (**some**) rice in the kitchen. I need (**a little**) more time.
Negative	There is**n't a** clock in the kitchen. There is **no** clock in the kitchen.	There are**n't** (**any**) windows in the kitchen. There are **no** windows in the kitchen.	There is**n't** (**any**) rice in the kitchen There's **no** rice in the kitchen.
Question	Is there **a** clock in the kitchen?	Are there (**any**) windows in the kitchen?	Is there (**any**) rice in the kitchen?

Language Notes: 1. *An* is used before singular count nouns that begin with a vowel.
I have *an* uncle, *an* aunt, and *a* grandmother.
2. *Some* and *any* can also be used in questions and alone.
Do you have *some* change? Do they need *any* volunteers?
3. Use an affirmative verb before *no*. Don't use the indefinite article after *no*.
There is *no* time.
There is *no* answer to your question.
There *isn't any* time.
There *isn't an* answer to your question.

■ **EXERCISE 1** Fill in each blank with *some*, *any*, *a*, *an*, or *no*.

Example Do you have _____any_____ money? I forgot my wallet today.

A. Do you have (1) _____any_____ milk that we could borrow?

We had (2) _____some_____ yesterday, but we drank it all.

Now we don't have (3) _____any_____, and we need

(4) _____some_____ for the baby's breakfast.

B. If we're going to the swimming pool, let's take (1) _____some_____

sunscreen. I like the kind with (2) _____a_____ high protection

level. I won't buy it if it doesn't have (3) _____any_____ sunscreen.

C. I can't go with you to the movies tonight because I have to write

(1) _____a_____ composition for one of my classes. In fact, I

have (2) _____some_____ homework for every class. I can't believe

you don't have (3) _____any_____ homework. You're really lucky!

■ **EXERCISE 2** Carol is going to make fish soup. The ingredients she doesn't need are crossed out. Make two lists: things Carol doesn't need (use *any* or *a / an* when listing each of these items) and things Carol needs to buy at the store (use *some* or *a / an* when listing each of these items).

Fabulous Fish Soup

½ cup olive oil	2 yellow onions	1 can tomato sauce
1 potato	1 large carrot	salt and pepper
2 teaspoons parsley	2 bay leaves	6 tablespoons butter
2 medium turnips	4 cups fish broth	3 pounds fish steaks
2 teaspoons flour		

Carol doesn't need:

Example _any olive oil_

1. _a Potato_
2. _any flour_
3. _any bay leaves_
4. _any salt and Pepper_
5. _any butter_

Carol needs:

Example _some parsley_

1. _some turnips_
2. _some onions_
3. _a Carrot_
4. _some fish broth_
5. _some / a can of tomato suce._
6. _some / several fish steaks_

■ **EXERCISE 3** Read the email and correct the mistakes. There are 8 mistakes.

Example There isn't ~~some~~ _any_ milk in the fridge.

To: william@english*school.com
Subject: We're Moving!

Hi William,

We're moving into some _a_ new apartment this weekend. Our old apartment had several problem! _Problems_

Whenever I took any _a_ shower, only _a_ little hot water came out. And ~~not~~ _no_ hot water at all came out after 10 a.m.!

The people living in our new building seem nice. Few _A few_ of them helped us move our boxes.

Unfortunately, there aren't an _any_ elevators in our new building, but that's OK.

If you have _some_ time next week, come see our new place. I'll send you the address later.

Carlos

	PLURAL COUNT	NONCOUNT
Affirmative	He has **a lot of** friends. He has **many** friends.	He has **a lot of** time.
Negative	He does**n't** have **many** friends. He does**n't** have **a lot of** friends.	He does**n't** have **much** time. He does**n't** have **a lot of** money.
Question	Does he have **many** friends? Does he have **a lot of** friends? How **many** friends does he have?	Does he have **much** time? Does he have **a lot of** time? How **much** time does he have?

a lot of = large quantity (No problem is presented.)	**too many / too much** = excessive quantity (A problem is presented.)
A lot of students study at the library. (**Many** students study at the library. They don't finish **much** work.) I have **a lot of** homework. I have **a lot of** cousins.	**Too many** students study at the library. The library is crowded and noisy. I have **too much** homework. I don't have time to talk to you. I have no time to study. I have **too many** family responsibilities.

Language Notes: 1. *Much* is rarely used in affirmative statements. It is more common to use *a lot of* in affirmative statements.
2. *A lot of* has a neutral tone. It shows a large quantity but doesn't present a problem. *Too much* or *too many* usually presents a problem or a complaint.
3. Use *too much* with noncount nouns. Use *too many* with count nouns.

■ **EXERCISE 1**   (Circle) the correct underlined word or words.

Example She can't eat many / (much) sugar.

1. Don't eat too much / too many oil or fat.
2. Humans need many / a little fat in their diet.
3. It's good to eat much / many vegetables every day.
4. We don't have much / several soda.
5. Do you eat much / many sugar?
6. Does he eat many / much cookies?
7. I have a little / a few friends with children.
8. The kids always have many / a lot of fun at the beach.
9. Their grandmother gave them a few / a little money for a snack.
10. They bought a lot of / much chocolate bars with the money.

■ **EXERCISE 2**   On the line, write *problem* if something excessive or bad is stated. Write *no problem* if no problem is presented.

Example   A few of my friends live near your house. _____*no problem*_____

1. I read a lot of books for school. __*No Problem*__
2. I spend too much time on the computer. __*Problems*__
3. You have several international friends. __*No Problem*__
4. We work too much. __*Problem*__
5. We have many assignments. __*no problem*__
6. She rests a lot. __*no problem*__
7. She drinks a lot of water. __*no problem*__
8. That costs a lot of money. __*no problem*__
9. It is too cloudy today. __*problem*__

■ **EXERCISE 3**   Write about your hometown. Use the quantity phrases (*a lot of, much, many, a little, a few, several*) to describe what your hometown has and doesn't have.

Example   My hometown doesn't have much crime. _____

_____

_____

_____

_____

■ **EXERCISE 4**   Read the paragraph and correct the mistakes. There are 6 mistakes.

Example   There ~~are~~ Is a radio in my car.

Yellowstone National Park

Come to Yellowstone National Park! There are ~~much~~ *a lot of/many* things you can do at the park. A lot *of*

visitors come to see Old Faithful, the famous geyser. There are ~~much~~ *a lot of/many* different kinds of animals you

can see—such as bears and wolves. Make sure you check the weather before you come. The park

gets ~~lot~~ *a lot* of snow in the winter. If you don't have ~~many~~ *a lot of/much* time, try a group tour. You can see much

things in a short period of time.

Practice 28 Adjectives

EXAMPLE	EXPLANATION
We ate a **big** meal. I don't like **fatty** foods.	An adjective describes a noun. An adjective can come before a noun.
Fast food is **inexpensive**. Models are **thin**. You look **healthy**. Hamburgers taste **delicious**.	An adjective can come after the verb *be* and the sense perception verbs (*look, seem, sound, smell, taste, feel*).
Are you **concerned** about your weight? I'm **tired** after work. The health club is **located** near my house.	Some *–ed* words are adjectives. For example: *concerned, tired, worried, crowded, located, married, divorced, excited, disappointed, finished, frightened.*
He exercised and **got tired**. I ran 3 miles and **got thirsty**. If you eat too much candy, you're going to **get sick**.	An adjective can follow *get* in these expressions: *get tired, get hungry, get sleepy, get thirsty, get worried, get married, get divorced, get sick, get angry.* In these expressions, *get* means *become*.

Language Notes: 1. We do not make adjectives plural:
a *thin* model; thin models   a *big* glass; big glasses
2. *Very, quite,* and *extremely* can come before adjectives:
You are *very* healthy.   They are *extremely* tired.

■ EXERCISE 1   Underline the adjective in each sentence or question.

Example That man seems <u>angry</u>.

1. We like to eat salad from a <u>wooden</u> bowl.
2. I love your dress! Was it <u>expensive</u>?
3. That television is <u>heavy</u>.
4. My <u>married</u> sister lives a few miles from here.
5. After the hike, they got <u>thirsty</u>.
6. The <u>blue</u> glass holds water.
7. I got <u>sick</u> before my meeting ended.
8. Why are you <u>worried</u> about your test?

■ EXERCISE 2   Write an appropriate adjective after the sense-perception verb.

Example Your hair looks _____**beautiful.**_____ Did you have it cut?

1. The river water felt _____ *cold* _____ on his bare feet.
2. My cooking tastes _____ *terrible* _____.

3. Ice cream tastes ___delicious___ .

4. This milk smells ___bad___ . Let's throw it out.

5. Your soup smells ___wonderful___ . What did you put in it?

6. The sky looks ___dark___ . I think it's going to rain.

7. Mother looks ___angry___ . Let's make dinner for her.

8. He seems ___tired___ . Did he have a bad day?

■ **EXERCISE 3** (Circle) the best adjective to complete each sentence.

Example She told me that her uncle owned a(n) (famous)/ awful restaurant.

1. I had fun! I took a boring / wonderful vacation last summer.

2. I was (excited)/ disappointed to leave on vacation.

3. I felt (disappointed)/ tired that I could only take a week off.

4. I spent most of my time on the (sunny)/ cloudy beaches.

5. I got (thirsty)/ angry on the hot beach.

6. She said that she liked undercooked /(gourmet) food.

7. She invited me to her uncle's restaurant for a (delicious)/ disgusting meal.

8. The restaurant was (crowded)/ empty.

9. A busy / nervous waiter took our order.

■ **EXERCISE 4** **Read the email and correct the mistakes. There are 6 mistakes.**

Example Many parks have ~~trails wooded~~ _wooded trails_ for hikers.

To: james.ronnie@africa*em.com

Subject: My Day

Dear Grandpa,

We went hiking last Saturday. It was so much fun! We went exploring in the forest dark. _dark forest._

Sometimes we had difficulty getting through the undergrowth thick. _thick_ Sometimes we almost got lost.

We kept going and were rewarded for our huges efforts. During our hike short through the woods, we

discovered many kinds of small animals. In the afternoon, we pitched a tent in a clearing beautiful.

We had a picnic delicious.

I will call you this weekend. I miss you!

James

Practice 29 Noun Modifiers

EXAMPLE	EXPLANATION
Do you have an **exercise machine**? A **farm worker** gets a lot of exercise. I joined a **health club**.	A noun can modify (describe) another noun. The second noun is more general than the first. *Strawberry jam* is a kind of jam; a *shoe store* is a kind of store.
I bought new **running shoes**. Do you ever use the **swimming pool**?	Sometimes a gerund (verb + –*ing*) describes a noun. It shows the purpose of the noun.
My **5-year-old** son prefers candy to fruit. **Potato chips** have a lot of grease. My new shoes are in the **shoebox**.	The first noun is always singular. A *5-year-old* son is a son who is 5 *years* old.
Do you have a **driver's license**? I don't understand the **owner's manual** for my new cell phone.	Sometimes a possessive form describes a noun.

■ **EXERCISE 1**　**Answer each question using one of the nouns in the question as a noun modifier. If the word is singular, use an article.**

Example　What kind of store can you buy shoes at? _____ *a shoe store* _____

1. What kind of government runs a city?

   _____

2. In what kind of class do you study biology?

   _____

3. At what kind of place do you wash cars?

   _____

4. What kind of doctor takes care of your eyes?

   _____

5. What kind of sale do stores have in the summer?

   _____

6. What do we call a person who stars in movies?

   _____

7. In what kind of garden do people grow vegetables?

   _____

8. What kind of salad has fruit in it?

   _____

9. What do you call a burger with cheese?

_____

10. What do you call a book full of telephone numbers?

_____

11. What do you call a child who is 10 years old?

_____

■ **EXERCISE 2** **Match the first noun (the noun modifier) with the second noun (the "main" noun) to create correct compound nouns.**

1. bed ————————————————— **a.** room

2. credit _Card_ **b.** table

3. living _room_ **c.** ball

4. tea _Cup_ **d.** boots

5. feather _Pillow_ **e.** water

6. book _bag._ **f.** card

7. kitchen _table_ **g.** pillow

8. base _ball_ **h.** room

9. rubber _boots_ **i.** cup

10. tap _water_ **j.** bag

■ **EXERCISE 3** **Read the paragraph and correct the mistakes. There are 5 mistakes.**

Example My sister finally learned how to drive. She got her ~~drive~~ _driver's_ license.

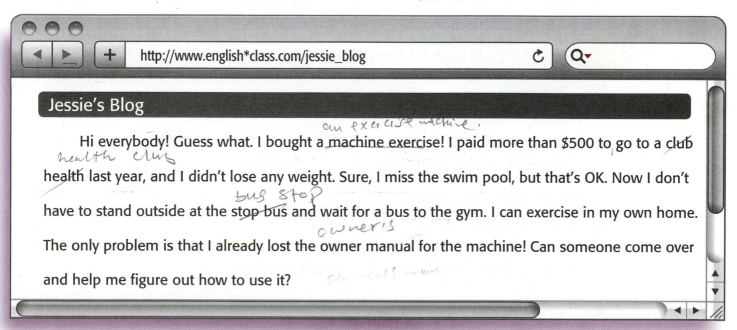

Jessie's Blog

Hi everybody! Guess what. I bought a ~~machine exercise~~ _an exercise machine._ I paid more than $500 to go to a club
health _health club_ last year, and I didn't lose any weight. Sure, I miss the swim pool, but that's OK. Now I don't

have to stand outside at the ~~stop bus~~ _bus stop_ and wait for a bus to the gym. I can exercise in my own home.

The only problem is that I already lost the owner _owner's_ manual for the machine! Can someone come over

and help me figure out how to use it?

EXAMPLE	EXPLANATION
I choose my food **carefully**. Some people eat **quickly**.	An adverb of manner tells how or in what way a person does something. We form most adverbs by adding –ly to the end of an adjective.
Do you eat **well**?	The adverb for *good* is *well*.
He worked **hard** and came home **late**. Don't eat so **fast**!	Some adverbs of manner do not end in –ly. The adjective and the adverb forms are the same.

Language Notes: 1. *Hard* and *hardly* are both adverbs, but they have different meanings:
He worked *hard*. = He put a lot of effort into his work.
He *hardly* worked. = He did very little work.
2. An adverb of manner usually follows the verb phrase:
She ate her lunch *quickly*. You speak English *well*.
3. *Very*, *extremely*, and *quite* can come before an adverb:
They work *very* slowly. She drives *extremely* well. You speak *quite* clearly.

■ **EXERCISE 1**   **Change the adjective into an adverb of manner.**

Example quick _____quickly_____

1. dangerous ___dangerously___   5. fast ___fast___
2. normal ___normally___   6. constant ___constantly___
3. safe ___safely___   7. slow ___slowly___
4. rapid ___rapidly___   8. good ___well___

■ **EXERCISE 2**   (Circle) **the adjective in the statement. Then write the adverb form of the adjective. Some adjectives and adverbs have the same form.**

Example I ate my food (quick.) _____quickly_____

1. I finished the work (easy.) ___easily___
2. They sold the house (cheap.) ___cheaply___
3. She waited for you (patient.) ___patiently___
4. I want to pronounce words (correct.) ___correctly___
5. He held the baby (careful.) ___carfully___
6. I didn't arrive late. ___late___
7. Make sure you eat slow. ___slowly___
8. They studied (hard) last night. ___heardd___
9. They don't celebrate birthdays (happy.) ___happily___
10. The teacher speaks good about her students. ___well___

■ **EXERCISE 3**   Insert *very*, *quite*, or *extremely* before the adverb.

Example   She studied <u>very</u> hard for the test.

1. She spoke Chinese *very* fluently.

2. He pushed his friend *extremely* roughly.

3. I completed my work carelessly.

4. They walked into the classroom *quite* quietly.

5. *Quite* Honestly, I am upset about the decision.

6. We completed our project *quite* thoughtfully.

7. You *very* politely asked me to wait with you.

8. The cat moves *extremely* silently in the night.

■ **EXERCISE 4**   **Read the letter and correct the mistakes. There are 8 mistakes.**

Example   The car ~~quick~~ *quickly* approached.

November 2nd

Dear Frank,

I real *really* love music. Every Friday after school, I go to the music store. I can hard *hardly* wait to see what new

CDs have arrived. I bicycle quick *quickly* to the store and join the other real *really* enthusiastic customers. I careful *carefully* stroll

through the aisles and slow *slowly* look at the CDs. When I know what I would like to buy, I patient *patiently* figure out which

items I can afford. Then I walk happy *happily* to the cash register.

Your friend,

Lily

ADJECTIVE	ADVERB
Jim looks **serious**. (*Serious* describes Jim.)	Jim is looking at his mistakes **seriously**. (*Seriously* describes how Jim is looking at his mistakes.)
Your composition looks **good**. (*Good* describes the composition.)	You wrote it **well**. (*Well* describes how you wrote it.)
My father was **angry**. (*Angry* describes my father.)	He spoke **angrily** to the children. (*Angrily* describes how he spoke to the children.)

Language Notes: 1. An adjective describes a noun (*happy* baby). An adverb describes a verb or verb phrase (walked *slowly*), an adjective (*well* written), or another adverb (*very* slowly).

2. Use an adjective after these verbs if you are describing the subject. Use an adverb if you are describing how the action (the verb) is done:

   smell   sound   seem   feel   taste   look   appear
   She *looks happy*.   She *is looking* at the contract *carefully*.

3. Use an adjective, not an adverb, in expressions with *get* or *become*:
   I got *cold* and *wet* in the rain.

■ **EXERCISE 1**   (Circle) the correct adjective or adverb.

Example You seem (happy) / happily today.

1. My sister is a wonderful / wonderfully cook.
2. She cooks extremely good / well.
3. Her Italian dishes taste particularly good / well.
4. She got excitedly / excited when she saw her sister get off the airplane.
5. They talked excited / excitedly until late into the night.
6. He became rich / richly from his Internet company.
7. He and his wife dance graceful / gracefully together.
8. My husband took me to a romantic / romantically movie.

■ **EXERCISE 2**   **Find the mistake in the underlined portion of the sentence. Rewrite the sentence correctly. If there is no mistake in the sentence, write *correct*.**

Example My father drives very <u>careful</u>.

<u>My father drives very carefully.</u>

1. He is a very <u>careful</u> driver.

_____Correct_____

2. I lost the race because I ran <u>slow</u>.

I lost the race because I ran slowly.

3. Sorry I'm late! My watch is <u>slow</u>.

Correct

4. He visits his parents in Brazil <u>frequent</u>.

He visits his parents in Brazil frequently.

5. That perfume smells <u>beautifully</u>.

That perfume smells beautiful

6. If you don't dress <u>quick</u>, we will be late.

If you don't dress quickly we will be late.

7. I hope I do <u>good</u> on my math test this week.

I hope I do well on my math test this week.

8. When I heard her message, I got <u>angrily</u>.

When I heard her message I got angry

9. If you work too <u>fast</u>, you might not do a good job.

Correct

10. Sandra appears <u>calm</u>, even though I know she is upset.

Correct

■ **EXERCISE 3   Read the paragraph and correct the mistakes. There are 6 mistakes.**

Example Cheryl sings Italian songs so ~~beautiful~~. *beautifully*

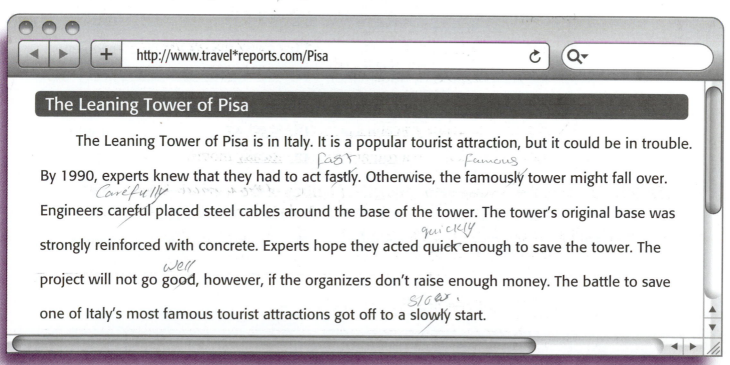

http://www.travel*reports.com/Pisa

The Leaning Tower of Pisa

The Leaning Tower of Pisa is in Italy. It is a popular tourist attraction, but it could be in trouble.

By 1990, experts knew that they had to act ~~fastly~~ *fast*. Otherwise, the ~~famously~~ *famous* tower might fall over.

Engineers ~~careful~~ *Carefully* placed steel cables around the base of the tower. The tower's original base was

strongly reinforced with concrete. Experts hope they acted ~~quick~~ *quickly* enough to save the tower. The

project will not go ~~good~~ *well*, however, if the organizers don't raise enough money. The battle to save

one of Italy's most famous tourist attractions got off to a ~~slowly~~ *slow*. start.

Practice 32 *Too* and *Enough*

TOO + ADJECTIVE; TOO + MUCH / MANY + NOUN	ADJECTIVE / ADVERB + ENOUGH	ENOUGH + NOUN
It's never **too late** to change your habits. Children eat **too much food** with lots of sugar. Children spend **too many hours** watching TV.	A diet of sodas and burgers is not **good enough**. I walked **quickly enough** to raise my heart rate.	I don't have **enough time** to exercise.

Language Notes:
1. *Too* indicates a problem. The problem is stated or implied.
2. Put *too* before the adjective or the adverb:
      too old   *too tired*   *too slowly*
3. Use *too much* before noncount nouns and *too many* before plural count nouns:
      too much time   *too many calories*
      too much grease   *too many sodas*
4. *Enough* means as much or as many as needed. Put *enough* after the adjective or adverb. Put *enough* before the noun:
      old enough   *tall enough*   *slowly enough*
      enough money   *enough time*   *enough books*
5. An infinitive phrase (*to* + base form of the verb) can follow a phrase with *too* and *enough*:
      He's too young *to understand* life.
      You're old enough *to drive*.

■ **EXERCISE 1** Write *too*, *too much*, or *too many* before each word.

Example _____too_____ loud

1. ___too many___ boxes
2. _____ small
3. _____ long
4. ___too much___ information
5. _____ hot
6. _____ expensive
7. ___too much___ sugar
8. _____ slowly
9. _____ ice
10. _____ carefully

11. _____ tired
12. _____ thin
13. ___too many___ problems
14. _____ heavy
15. _____ difficult
16. _____ simple
17. _too many / too much_ fish
18. ___too much___ money
19. _____ hard
20. ___too many___ people

■ **EXERCISE 2** Write *enough* before or after the word.

Example Is the classroom _____ quiet _____ enough _____ to study?

1. Are the children _____ old _____ enough _____ to go to camp?

2. Did I cut the string _____ short _____ enough _____?

3. You gave me _____ enough _____ advice _____.

4. We think that car is _____ cheap _____ enough _____.

5. The cook put _____ enough _____ salt _____ in the soup.

6. I think there is _____ enough _____ hot water _____ for a shower.

7. They had _____ enough _____ hope _____ to try calling again.

8. Are you _____ tired _____ enough _____ to sleep well tonight?

9. They drive _____ carefully _____ enough _____ at night.

10. Are there _____ enough _____ books _____ on Brazilian history?

11. There is _____ enough _____ meat _____ for the whole family to eat.

12. Are there _____ enough _____ forks _____ on the table for six people?

■ **EXERCISE 3** Read the paragraph and correct the mistakes. There are 7 mistakes.

Example There are ~~many too~~ *too many* people in the hallway.

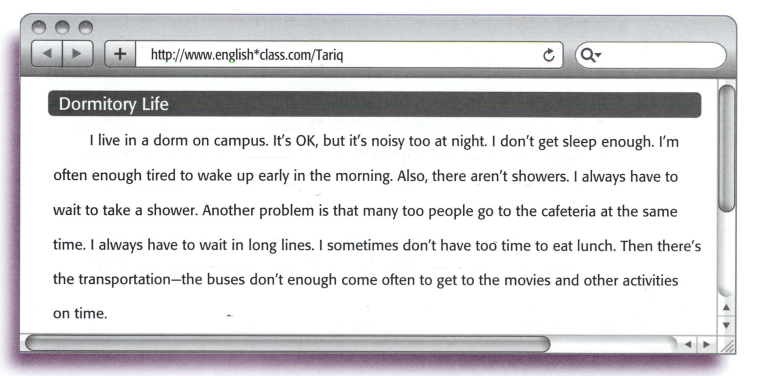

Dormitory Life

I live in a dorm on campus. It's OK, but it's noisy too at night. I don't get sleep enough. I'm

often enough tired to wake up early in the morning. Also, there aren't showers. I always have to

wait to take a shower. Another problem is that many too people go to the cafeteria at the same

time. I always have to wait in long lines. I sometimes don't have too time to eat lunch. Then there's

the transportation—the buses don't enough come often to get to the movies and other activities

on time.

Practice 33 *Very* and *Too*

SUBJECT	VERB	*VERY / TOO*	ADJECTIVE OR ADVERB
That computer	is	**very**	expensive, but I have enough money.
That computer	is	**too**	expensive for me to buy.
I	was	**very**	tired, but I went to work.
I	was	**too**	tired to exercise after work.
She	speaks	**very**	quickly.
You	speak	**too**	quickly. I can't understand you.

Language Note: Don't confuse *very* and *too*. *Very* is a neutral word. *Too* always indicates a problem in a specific situation. The problem can be stated or implied.

■ **EXERCISE 1** Match the comments of Speaker A with the responses of Speaker B.

Speaker A

1. Why can't he vote? _____a_____
2. How old is her son? ___e___
3. What's the weather like outside? ___h___
4. Why don't you want to work in the garden this weekend? ___g___
5. Why can't we get this bookcase in the truck? ___f___
6. What do you like best about flowers? ___b___
7. Why did you leave so early? ___d___
8. Do you want to hike to the lake? ___i___
9. Why are you working so late tonight? ___j___
10. Are you coming with me to the movie? ___c___

Speaker B

a. He's too young.
b. They smell very sweet.
c. No, I'm too busy.
d. It's very far.
e. He's very young.
f. It's too tall.
g. It's too wet.
h. It's very hot today.
i. No, it's too far.
j. I'm very busy.

■ **EXERCISE 2** Fill in the blank with *too* or *very*.

Example I won't let my daughter wear makeup because she's _____too_____ young.

1. I can't keep up with you. You're walking _____too_____ fast.
2. That box is _____too_____ heavy for me to lift.
3. The belt is _____too_____ big for me. It's falling off.
4. She speaks _____very_____ slowly so we can understand everything.

5. It's ___*very*___ cold out today. Make sure you wear a coat.

6. It's ___*too*___ hot to wear a coat today.

7. It's ___*too*___ late to call them. They're probably asleep.

8. I'm ___*very*___ full, but I can still eat dessert!

■ **EXERCISE 3**   Finish the sentence with *too* or *very* + an adjective from the box.

Example I'm going to bed early tonight. I'm ___*very tired*___.

tired	sick	difficult	angry	sad	hot
sunny	sour	boring	cloudy	valuable	

1. Pass me the sugar, please. This lemonade is ___*too / very sour*___

2. After the operation, the man got better, but he was still ___*very sick*___.

3. When I told my boss about my mistake, she was ___*very angry*___.

4. I didn't finish the homework because it was ___*too / very difficult*___

5. Let's go cheer Jane up. She looks ___*very sad*___.

6. Let your soup cool off a minute. It's ___*too / very hot*___.

7. This weather is perfect for a picnic! It's ___*very sunny*___.

8. Please be careful when you wash that vase. It is ___*very valuable*___

9. I went to sleep during the movie. It was ___*very boring*___.

10. They didn't go swimming at the beach. It was ___*very / too cloudy*___

■ **EXERCISE 4**   Read the email and correct the mistakes. There are 6 mistakes.

Example The book ~~very is~~ funny! *is very*

To: maria@english*class.com

Subject: My English Class

Hi Maria,

   I just graduated to the next level in my English program. I'm ~~too~~ *very* excited about my progress.

My English is getting better! My new teacher is ~~nice very~~ *very nice*, but she ~~too quickly speaks~~ *speaks too quickly*. It's ~~hard very~~ *very hard* to

understand her. She also gives us too much homework, but I'm learning a lot. My new classmates are

~~too~~ *very* interesting. I'm making some new friends. I ~~very~~ miss you *very* much! Don't wait too long to write back.

I want to hear how you are!

Rosa

TIME WORD	EXAMPLE	EXPLANATION
for	He talked on the phone **for** one hour.	*For* tells how long.
in	I finished the job **in** May 2010.	Use *in* with a specific year or month.
	I finished the job **in** five days.	Use *in* to mean after or within a period of time.
during	We visited Angkor Wat **during** our trip to Cambodia.	Use *during* with an activity.
by	You must renew your passport **by** July.	*By* means no later than.
ago	We moved into our house three years **ago**.	*Ago* means before now.

Language Notes: 1. Compare *before* and *ago*:
    Yoko got a job *before* she graduated. Yoko got a job three years *ago*.
2. Compare *during* and *for*:
    Pavel fell asleep *during* the movie. Pavel slept *for* two hours.
3. Compare *after* and *in*:
    I'll come back *in* an hour. I'll come back *after* I go swimming.
4. Compare *before* and *by*:
    We have to return the library books *before* Friday. (Friday is not included.)
    We have to return the library books *by* Friday. (Friday is included.)

■ **EXERCISE 1**　Fill in the blank with *during* or *for*.

Example I was asleep _____during_____ class.

1. Something woke her up ____during____ the night.
2. They drove ____for____ 13 hours before they stopped.
3. Your name came up ____during____ our conversation.
4. The astronauts remained in orbit ____for____ 41 days.
5. It rains a lot here ____during____ the winter months.
6. ____during____ the war, he fought in many battles.
7. I think you should stay in bed ____for____ a few days.
8. The children become restless ____during____ long car trips.

■ **EXERCISE 2**　Fill in the blank with *ago* or *in*.

Example I learned to do the job _____in_____ five days.

1. We love to visit the park ____in____ the spring.
2. The twins were born four years ____ago____.
3. You'd better hurry. The plane leaves ____in____ 30 minutes.

4. A few days _____ago_____, she got a telephone call that changed her life.

5. I always do my best work _____in_____ the morning.

6. Why don't we travel somewhere _____in_____ August?

■ EXERCISE 3   Fill in each blank with *by* or *in*.

Example He will lose five pounds _____by_____ October.

1. She has to be at the office _____by_____ 8:30 every day.

2. I will complete my homework _____in_____ three hours.

3. If you'll help me, we can finish _____by_____ noon.

4. _____in_____ a few hours, they will leave.

5. Fortunately the rain had stopped _____by_____ the time I left the building.

6. _____in_____ January, I am going to return to China.

■ EXERCISE 4   Read the Web page and correct the mistakes. There are 6 mistakes.

Example I went there ~~ago~~ September <u>in</u> for 3 days.

http://www.travel*ATX.com/Dante

New Orleans Trip!

Hey friends!

We are planning a trip to visit New Orleans. We are going with *to* a tour group. Here's what you need to know:

- We are leaving *in* for 6 weeks. Today is March 19th, so that means we will leave on April 30th.

- We will stay there *for* in 5 days and 4 nights. We'll come back on May 4th. We will see many amazing things *during* by our tour.

- The cost is $300. We need to pay *by* for April 2nd.

You won't want to miss this trip! I went to New Orleans *in* ago 2007. It was awesome! Please let me know if you're coming *by* in March 26th. It's going to be so much fun!

Practice 35 Past Continuous Tense

EXAMPLE	EXPLANATION
Last night I **was watching** the late show on TV. My roommates **were watching** it with me.	To form the past continuous tense, we use *was* or *were* + gerund (base form + –*ing*): *I / he / she / it* → *was* + gerund *you / we / they* → *were* + gerund
I **was not sleeping**. My roommates **weren't paying** attention.	To form the negative, put *not* after *was* or *were*. The contraction for *was not* is *wasn't*. The contraction for *were not* is *weren't*.
Was he **living** in the United States? Yes, he **was**. / No, he **wasn't**. Where **was** he **living**? Who **was living** in Germany?	*Yes / no* question Short answer *Wh*– question *Wh*– (subject)

■ **EXERCISE 1** Write the past continuous form of the verb to tell about events that were happening around the world yesterday.

Example (rain) It _____was raining_____ in the Nile River valley.

1. (snow) It __was snowing__ in the Himalayas.
2. (try) People __were trying__ to climb Mount Everest.
3. (take) Students __were taking__ English entrance exams.
4. (think) A young man in Thailand __was thinking__ about his sweetheart.
5. (wonder) His sweetheart __was wondering__ if he loved her.
6. (break) In the Arctic, an iceberg __was breaking__ free.
7. (worry) A mother in Nigeria __was worrying__ about her son.
8. (enjoy) A Russian journalist __was enjoying__ his vacation.

■ **EXERCISE 2** Unscramble the words and phrases to make a past continuous question.

Example speaking to / who / she / on the phone / was

Who was she speaking to on the phone?

1. were / to my advice / listening / you

   You were listening to my advice.

2. playing / was / where / last night / the guitar / he

   Where was he Playing the guitar last night?

3. was / who / with him / singing

   Who was singing with him?

4. in the afternoon / he / reading / a book / wasn't

Wasn't he reading a book in the afternoon?

5. was / she / after work / what / yesterday / doing

What was she doing after work yesterday?

■ **EXERCISE 3** Write a sentence about what you and your friends *were* or *weren't* doing last night.

Example (I / exercise) <u>I wasn't exercising last night.</u>

1. (my friends / study English)

my friends weren't study English.

2. (I / speak on the phone)

I wasn't speaking on the phone.

3. (I / write a letter)

I wasn't writing a letter?

4. (I / speak on the phone)

I wasn't speaking on the phone

5. (my friends / cook a big dinner)

my friends were cooking a big dinner.

■ **EXERCISE 4** Read the conversation and correct the mistakes. There are 4 mistakes.

Example She ~~slept~~ *was sleeping* when the doorbell rang.

Carlos: How was your camping trip?

Jean: It was awful.

Carlos: What happened?

Jean: First of all, while we were ~~set up~~ *setting up* our tents, it got really windy. Everything *was* blowing all over the place!

Carlos: What else happened?

Jean: Then, when we *were* trying to cook over the campfire, it started to rain.

Carlos: That sounds terrible!

Jean: Yeah, it was. We *were* thinking of going camping again next month, but I think we'll stay home instead!

EXAMPLE	EXPLANATION
What **were** you **doing** at 10 o'clock yesterday morning? I **was working** in the computer lab.	We use the past continuous tense to show what was in progress at a specific moment in the past.
The cashier **was counting** the money when the robbers **entered** the store. While the robbers **were taking** the money, the cashier **pushed** the alarm button.	We use the past continuous tense with the simple past tense to show the relationship of a longer past action to a shorter past action.

Language Notes: 1. You can show the relationship of a longer past action to a shorter past action in two ways:
  - Use *when* + simple past tense with the shorter action.
      The cashier was counting the money *when* the robbers *entered* the store.
  - Use *while* + past continuous tense with the longer action.
      While the robbers *were taking* the money, the cashier pushed the alarm button.
2. If the time clause precedes the main clause, separate the two clauses with a comma:

TIME CLAUSE	**MAIN CLAUSE**
When he died,	he was living in the city.

MAIN CLAUSE	**TIME CLAUSE**
He was living in the city	when he died.

■ **EXERCISE 1** **Rewrite the sentence using a past continuous or simple past verb. Check the sentence for correct comma use.**

Example (while / I / walk) it started to rain.

  While I was walking, it started to rain.

1. I was working on the computer (when / the electricity / go off).

  I was working on the Computer when the electricity went off

2. Another car hit mine (when / I / stop) at the red light.

  Another car hit mine when I was stopping at the red light

3. (while / my sister / have) a party, my cousins came to visit.

  While my sister was having a party, my cousins came to visit.

4. (while / he / ski) on the mountain, he broke his leg.

  While he was skiing on the mountain, he broke his leg.

5. The telephone rang (while / we / eat) dinner.

  The telephone rang, will we were eating dinner.

6. We found a lot of wildflowers (while / we / hike).

  We found a lot of wildflowers, while we were hiking.

7. (when / you / come over), I was watching a DVD.

When you came over, I was watching a DVD Per noon?

8. She was working at the clothing store (when / you / see) her for the first time.

She was working at the clothing store, When you saw her for the   *First time*

9. (when / you / call) me on the phone, the children were talking loudly.

When you called me on the Phone, the children were talking loudly.

10. I read my book (while / the children / sleep).

I read my book, while the children were sleeping.

11. He fell off the horse (while / he / ride) across the field.

He fell off the horse while he was rideing across the field.

12. (when / I / arrive) at the doctor's office, many patients were waiting.

When I arrived at the doctor's office, many Patients were waiting.

■ EXERCISE 2   Answer the question (*What did you do? / What were you doing?*) using the simple past or the past continuous tense.

Example While I was preparing dinner, <u>my husband helped me chop vegetables.</u>

1. When it started to rain, I _____.

2. While I was eating dinner, I _____.

3. When my friend came to visit, I _____.

4. While my friends were studying, I _____.

5. When I went to the bank, I _____.

6. While I was cleaning the kitchen, _____.

7. When I wrote you a letter, _____.

8. While I was doing the laundry, _____.

■ EXERCISE 3   Read the note and correct the mistakes. There are 10 mistakes.

Example While I was reading, I ~~fall~~ *fell* asleep.

While I was ~~do~~ *doing* my laundry, I ~~hear~~ *heard* a noise. When I ~~turning~~ *turned* around, I ~~see~~ *saw* that the door was open. Chills

ran up and down my back. I quietly ~~walk~~ *walked* around the corner when I heard the sound of an animal. The animal

~~jump~~ *jumped* out at me while I was ~~take~~ *taking* a closer look at it. When it ~~do~~ *did* that, I jumped too and ~~starting~~ *starting* screaming.

That was when I ~~wake up~~ *woke up*.

Practice 37 *Was / Were going to*

WAS / WERE GOING TO (THE PLAN)	BUT . . . (WHY THE PLAN DIDN'T HAPPEN)
We **were going to** visit you,	but our car broke down.
He **was going to** give his daughter the good news,	but somebody else told her first.

Language Note: We use *was / were going to* + the base form of the verb to describe a plan that we didn't carry out. It means the same thing as *was / were planning to* + the base form of the verb.

■ EXERCISE 1   Complete the sentence with the missing word or verb.

Example We were _____ *going* _____ to meet you yesterday, but I got sick.

1. He _____ *was* _____ going to call you, but he had a lot of homework.

2. You were going to _____ *do* _____ your homework, but you forgot.

3. They _____ *were* _____ going to study for the exam, but they lost their notes.

4. She was going to go to the dentist, but _____ *she* _____ didn't have enough time.

5. They were going _____ *to* _____ save some cake for you, but they ate the last piece.

6. _____ *He* _____ was going to bring us lunch, but he left it on the bus.

7. She _____ *was* _____ going to clean her room, but she ran out of time.

8. You were going _____ *to* _____ water the plants, but you fed the cat first.

■ EXERCISE 2   Complete the sentence with a plan expressed with *was / were going to*.

Example _____ *I was going to buy you a present* _____, but I didn't know what you want.

1. _____, but you interrupted me.

2. _____, but it started to rain.

3. _____, but my parents wouldn't let me.

4. _____, but I had too much to do.

5. _____, but I changed my mind.

6. _____, but just then the phone rang.

7. _____, but it was too hot.

8. _____, but my friends
   wanted to go home.

9. _____, but it was easier
   to do it by email.

10. _____, but my boss asked
    me to do something else instead.

■ **EXERCISE 3**   Respond to the sentence by writing a complete sentence with
was / were going to, but. . . .

Example   You didn't mail these bills.

<u>I was going to mail them, but the post office was closed.</u>

1. You didn't meet me at the train station.

   _____

2. You never told me you had an accident with the car.

   _____

3. Why didn't you buy a gift for the bride and groom?

   _____

4. You didn't pay your credit card bill.

   _____

5. You didn't make a doctor's appointment.

   _____

■ **EXERCISE 4**   Read the conversation and correct the mistakes. There are 6 mistakes.

Example   Dwayne's mother ~~were~~ ^{was} going to drive to work, but she had a flat tire.

Ming: Hi Mom! I thought you were going go shopping!

Mom: I was to go, but the store was closed.

Ming: Closed! What were going to buy?

Mom: I were going to look for a new sweater for the party.

Ming: I thought you was going to wear the blue one.

Mom: I was going wear that one, but it is stained.

Ming: That's too bad, Mom.

Overview of Modals and Related Expressions

MODALS	FACTS ABOUT MODALS

can
would
could
should
will
may
might
must
	1. The base form of the verb follows a modal. Never use an infinitive after a modal:
	      You **must pay** your rent. [**Not:** You must to pay your rent.]
	2. Modals never have an –s, –ed, or –ing ending:
	      He **can** go. [**Not:** He cans go.]
	3. To form the negative, put *not* after the modal:
	      You **should not** leave now.
	4. You can make a negative contraction with some modals:
	    can't *wouldn't* *couldn't*
	    shouldn't *won't* *mustn't*
	5. Some verbs are like modals in meaning: *have to, had better, ought to, be able to, be supposed to, be permitted to, be allowed to*:
	      He **must** sign the lease. = He **has to** sign the lease.

■ **EXERCISE 1**   **Read the statement and <u>underline</u> the modal or the verb that acts as a modal. (See item 5 in the chart above.)**

Example In some countries, people <u>are supposed to</u> keep dogs on leashes.

1. A successful dog trainer <u>has to</u> keep several things in mind.

2. A proverb says, "You <u>can't</u> teach an old dog new tricks."

3. This proverb <u>may not</u> always be true, but it certainly is easier to train a puppy than an older dog.

4. First, you <u>must</u> develop a good relationship with the puppy.

5. Next, you <u>have to</u> make sure that the puppy understands your signals.

6. Of course, the puppy <u>should not be permitted to</u> run wild.

7. A young dog <u>ought to</u> learn how to sit up, roll over, shake hands, and fetch a stick.

8. The trainer <u>should</u> praise the dog when it performs a trick correctly.

9. Some dogs <u>will</u> learn faster than others.

10. You <u>shouldn't</u> punish your dog if it <u>can't</u> learn quickly.

11. You <u>must</u> try to figure out what the problem is.

12. Children <u>might</u> like the responsibility of a pet.

13. They <u>may be allowed to</u> feed, groom, and walk the dog.

■ **EXERCISE 2**   (Circle) the correctly formed modal.

Example   He willn't / (won't) help train the dog.

1. Humans can training / train dogs to do tricks.
2. You (can't) / can't to teach an old dog new tricks.
3. This proverb mays / (may) not always be true.
4. You are supposed to (make) / making sure that the puppy understands your signals.
5. The puppy must does / (do) what you want, too.
6. Dogs (aren't able) / aren't able to concentrate for as long as you.
7. A young dog may to learn / (learn) a few simple tricks within a week.
8. The dog have to / (has to) enjoy the lessons.
9. Soon the dog will know / knowing your commands.
10. Don't punish your dog if he can't / can to learn quickly.
11. You maybe / (might) come to the conclusion that your dog just isn't a fast learner.
12. Both you and your pet will to / (will be) happier if the dog receives a lot of praise.

■ **EXERCISE 3**   **Read the email and correct the mistakes. There are 6 mistakes.**

Example   You should not ~~to~~ quit your job before you have a new one.

To:	leon@my*line.com
Subject:	Your Job

Hi Leon!

I know you want to quit your job, but you should to find another job first. You maybe decide that

getting a new job is a good idea, but you are could be left with no job if you no can find another one.

You cans get a better job, but you might to have to wait a little longer.

Love,

Dad

WH–WORD	MODAL (+ N'T)	SUBJECT	MODAL (+ N'T)	VERB	COMPLEMENT	SHORT ANSWER
		He	**can**	**have**	a cat in his apartment.	
		He	**can't**	**have**	a dog.	
	Can	he		**have**	a bird?	No, he **can't**. /
What	**can**	he		**have**	in his apartment?	Yes, he **can**.
Why	**can't**	he		**have**	a dog?	
		Who	**can**	**have**	pets in their apartment?	

■ **EXERCISE 1**   **Make a question with the modal or expression and subject in parentheses.**

Example Q: (can / who) _____ *Who can* _____ show us the way to the theater?

A: Harry can.

1. **Q:** (we / should) _*Should we*_ _____ leave the baby here while we shop?

   A: No, we can't do that.

2. **Q:** (why / we / not / could) _*Why could not we*_ ___ fix the broken printer?

   A: It is too complicated. We need to call an expert.

3. **Q:** (must / I / where) _*Where must I*_ ___ pay for this overdue book?

   A: At the main desk.

4. **Q:** (people / how many / may) _*How many people may*_ be in this car at one time?

   A: No more than five.

5. **Q:** (has to / who) _*Who has to*_ ___ clean the house today?

   A: We do, unfortunately.

6. **Q:** (be able to / you) _*Are you be able to*_ swim the length of the pool five times?

   A: No, I can't. Ask someone else.

7. **Q:** (might / when / you) _*When might you*_ ___ come over?

   A: Just as soon as I finish what I'm doing.

8. **Q:** (be supposed to / who) _*Who is supposed to*_ ___ give him the bad news?

   A: I think you ought to.

■ **EXERCISE 2**   Unscramble the words to make a question with a modal expression.

Example   the homework / hand in / tomorrow / I / may

May I hand in the homework tomorrow?

1. the hospital / permitted / when / you / to leave / are

   When are you Permitted to leave the hospital?

2. I / this purchase / a credit card / pay for / with / can

   Can I pay for this Purchase with a credit card?

3. ought to / for / who / pay / dinner

   Who ought to pay for dinner?

4. without / to travel / people / why / allowed / a passport / aren't

   Why arn't people allowed to travel without a Passport?

5. able / graduate / when / she / to / will / be

   When she will be able to graduate?

6. a car / must / drive / how old / you / to / be

   How old you must be to drive?

■ **EXERCISE 3**   Read the conversation and correct the mistakes. There are 6 mistakes.

Example   He ~~no can~~ ^{can't} have a dog at home because it makes him sneeze.

Sam: What ~~he can~~ ^{can he} have for snack?

Mom: He ^{can} have juice.

Sam: ^{Can he} He ~~can~~ have some cake?

Mom: No, he should ^{shouldn't} ~~no~~ have any cake.

Sam: Why shouldn't he ~~no~~ have any cake?

Mom: He might ~~to~~ get sick.

_he_

Practice 40 *Must, Have to, Have got to, and Be supposed to*

FORMAL / OFFICIAL	INFORMAL	USE
Everyone **must** obey the law.	Everyone **has to** obey the law. Everyone **has got to** obey the law. Everyone **is supposed to** obey the law.	Legal obligation
We **must** operate on him immediately.	We **have to** operate on him immediately. We**'ve got to** operate on him immediately.	Urgency
I **have to** wash my car.	I**'ve got to** wash my car.	Personal necessity

Language Notes: 1. We don't usually use *have got to* for questions or negatives.
2. *Must* has no past form. The past of both *must* and *have to* is *had to*.

■ **EXERCISE 1** Fill in the blank with *must* for rules and laws. Fill in the blank with *have / has to* or *have / has got to* for personal necessities and urgent situations.

Example Taxpayers _____**must**_____ mail their tax forms by April 15th.

1. I _'ve got to_ pick up some milk on my way home.
2. I'm so tired. I _have to_ start going to bed earlier.
3. Students _must_ pay their fees by the last day of January.
4. We _have to_ get to the bank before it closes.
5. Swimmers _must_ not bring glass bottles into the pool area.
6. Employees _must_ wash their hands before returning to work.
7. I _'ve got to_ find a part-time job to earn some money.
8. Pedestrians _must_ cross the street at the crosswalk.
9. I _'ve got to_ give you back your book.
10. Students _must_ not eat in the library.
11. We _have to_ pay her back.
12. I _'ve got to_ buy my mother a birthday present.

■ **EXERCISE 2** Complete each sentence. Use an appropriate verb.

Example Parents have to _protect their children._

1. In the summer, students don't have to _____.
2. Every car owner has to _____.
3. A good teacher is supposed to _____.
4. Every landlord has got to _____.

5. People who live in a dormitory don't have to _____.

6. Police officers mustn't _____.

7. Retired people don't have to _____.

8. Athletes in training are supposed to _____.

■ **EXERCISE 3** **Complete the sentence by telling what you and other people *must, have to, have got to*, and *are supposed to* do in life.**

Example I have to <u>study every night.</u> _____

1. People have to _____.

2. I have got to _____.

3. I must _____.

4. Children must _____.

5. They are supposed to _____.

■ **EXERCISE 4** **Read the email and correct the mistakes. There are 7 mistakes.**

Example I've got ^to pick up my brother after work.

To: mama@home*base.com

Subject: A Problem

Hi Mom!

What should I do? I have ^to study today. I've get to get an A on this test. But I ^I am supposed to meet

Julie for dinner. I ^I am supposed to call her soon. I'll just have ^to tell her I can't meet her tonight. Julie has

gotten ^got to understand. That's what friends are suppose to do. Right?

Love,

Me

MODAL	ALTERNATIVE EXPRESSION	USE
She **can** pay up to $500 for her plane ticket.	**It is possible** for her to pay up to $500 for her plane ticket.	Possibility
I **can't** open the door. I **can** speak three languages.	I **am not able to** open the door. I **am able to** speak three languages.	Ability
We **can't** take more than two bags on the plane.	We **are not permitted to / are not allowed to** take more than two bags on the plane.	Permission
You **may** leave whenever you want to.	You **are allowed to / are permitted to** leave whenever you want to.	Permission
I **couldn't** operate a computer three years ago, but now I **can**.	I **wasn't able to** operate a computer three years ago, but now I **am able to**.	Past ability
I **couldn't** drive until I got a license, but now I **can**.	I **wasn't permitted to** drive until I got a license, but now I **am permitted to / am allowed to**.	Past permission

■ **EXERCISE 1** **Underline** the modal expression and change it to the negative past tense.

Example He <u>can</u> pay his credit card bill today.

(last week) <u>**He couldn't pay his credit card bill last week.**</u>

1. Amy <u>can</u> play the flute very well this year.

(last year) *Amy couldn't play the flute very well last year.*

2. Janet is allowed to borrow books from the library this week.

(last week) *Janet wasnot/wasn't allowed to borrow books from the library last week.*

3. We are <u>able</u> to play soccer as a team this month.

(two months ago) *We werenot/weren't able to play soccer a team two months a goo*

4. It is possible for Eric to earn a lot of money in this job.

(in his previous job) *It wasnot/wasn't possible for Eric to earn a lot of money in his previous job.*

5. They <u>may</u> live in the dormitories this term.

(last term) *They were not/weren't allowed to live in the dormitories last term.*

■ **EXERCISE 2** **Underline** the modal or modal expression and write an alternative expression in its place.

Example I <u>can't</u> pay $1,200 a year for car insurance.

<u>**It isn't possible for me to pay $ 1,200 a year for car insurance.**</u>

1. My sister <u>can</u> babysit on Saturday nights.

   It is not Possible for my sister to babysit on saturday

2. The children may watch TV until 9:00 p.m.

   The children are Permitted to watch TV until 9:00 p.m.

3. I could sing very well when I was young, but now I can't.

   I was able to sing very well when I was young, but now I am not _able to r_

4. It isn't possible for me to take a vacation any time soon.

   I can't take a vacation any time soon.

5. The little boy wasn't allowed to stay up late, but now he is.

   The little boy couldn't stay up late, But now he can.

6. The runner wasn't able to reduce his speed this year.

   The runner couldn't reduce his speed last Year.

■ **EXERCISE 3** **Read the Web page and correct the mistakes. There are 6 mistakes.**

   Example I wasn't able _to_ work last semester, but I can now.

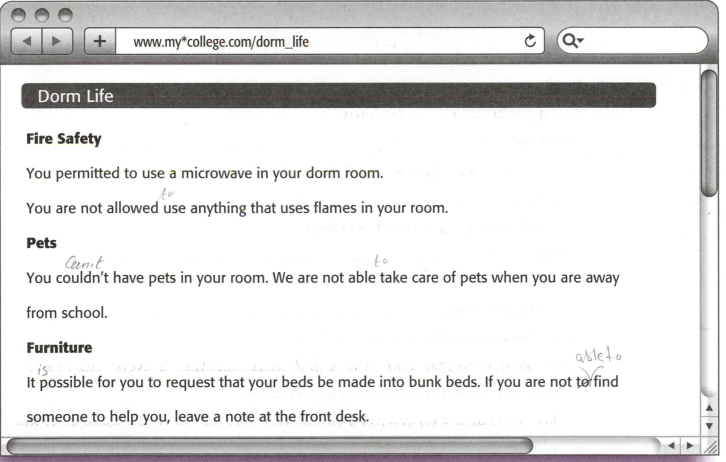

Dorm Life

Fire Safety

You permitted to use a microwave in your dorm room.

You are not allowed _to_ use anything that uses flames in your room.

Pets

can't
You couldn't have pets in your room. We are not able _to_ take care of pets when you are away

from school.

Furniture

_is_
It possible for you to request that your beds be made into bunk beds. If you are not _able to_ find

someone to help you, leave a note at the front desk.

Practice 42 *Should* and *Had better*

EXAMPLE	EXPLANATION
You **should** talk to a counselor about your problem. You **shouldn't** get so upset.	For advice, use *should*: *should* = It's a good idea. *shouldn't* = It's a bad idea.
You **had better** renew your visa before you leave the country. You **had better not** forget to do it, or you won't be able to get back in.	For a warning, use *had better* (*not*). Something bad might happen if you don't follow this advice.

Language Note: The contraction for *had* (in *had better*) is *'d*:
  I'd   you'd   he'd   she'd   we'd   they'd

■ **EXERCISE 1**   Label the sentence: *This is good advice.* or *This is a warning.*

Examples We should ask the doctor about vitamins.   <u>This is good advice.</u>

You'd better not be impolite to your boss.   <u>This is a warning.</u>

1. You should see the dentist about your toothache.

   This is good advice

2. We had better not eat any more junk food.

   This is warning.

3. He should buy groceries on his way home tonight.

   This is good advice.

4. I'd better not leave my cell phone in the car again.

   This is warning.

■ **EXERCISE 2**   Rewrite the affirmative sentence as a negative sentence, or rewrite the negative sentence as an affirmative sentence.

Example You had better not drive slowly. <u>You'd better drive slowly.</u>

1. You'd better stay up all night before the test.

   You'd better not stay up all night before the test.

2. Susannah should arrive late to work every day.

   Susannah shouldn't/should not arrive late to work every day.

3. We'd better not do our laundry this week.

   We'd better do our laundry this week.

4. I had better gain more weight.

   I had better not gain more weight.

EXERCISE 3 Your friend is traveling to another country. Choose 4 expressions from the box. Then give your friend advice using *should* (for good or bad ideas) or *had better* (for legal necessities or warnings). Some sentences can be negative.

Example <u>You had better make a doctor's appointment.</u>

apply for a passport	take a bilingual dictionary	lose your airplane tickets
~~make a doctor's appointment~~	give your family an emergency telephone number	change some money
get a visa		take some gifts for people there
pack your swimsuit	take an umbrella	

What should your friend do?

1. _____

2. _____

3. _____

4. _____

EXERCISE 4 Read the conversation and correct the mistakes. There are 5 mistakes.

Example You ~~shouldnt~~ ^{shouldn't} close the door so hard.

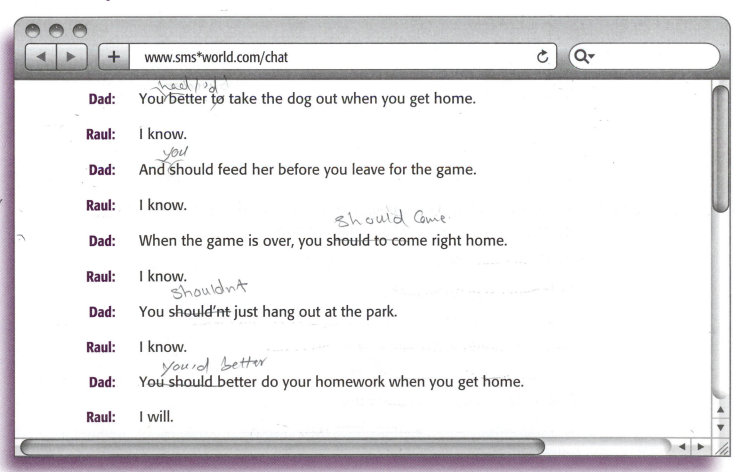

Dad: You *had/'d* better ~~to~~ take the dog out when you get home.

Raul: I know.

Dad: And *you* should feed her before you leave for the game.

Raul: I know.

Dad: When the game is over, you ~~should to come~~ *should come* right home.

Raul: I know.

Dad: You ~~should'nt~~ *shouldn't* just hang out at the park.

Raul: I know.

Dad: ~~You should better~~ *You'd better* do your homework when you get home.

Raul: I will.

Practice 43 Negatives of Modals and Related Expressions

EXAMPLE	EXPLANATION
Passengers **must not** remove their seatbelts at this time.	Use *must not* for a prohibition. These things are against the law or rules. (*Must not* sounds official.)
I **cannot** have a dog in my apartment. You **may not** use a calculator on the test.	Use *cannot* or *may not* to show no permission. The meaning is similar to *must not.*
You**'re not supposed to** park here.	Use *be not supposed to* for a prohibition. These things are against the law or rules.
You **are not supposed to** drive quickly near schools or in the city.	When reporting a rule, we use *be not supposed to* more often than *must not.* (Remember, *must not* sounds official.)
She **doesn't have to** take the entrance examination because she doesn't want to go to college.	A person can perform a particular action if he or she wants to, but he or she has no obligation to do it.
You **shouldn't** watch so much TV.	*Shouldn't* is for advice, not rules.
You**'d better not** miss the final exam, or you'll fail the course.	*Had better not* is for a warning.

Language Note: *Ought to* is used in affirmative statements. Do not use this expression in negative statements or questions.

■ **EXERCISE 1** Circle the best negative modal to complete the sentence.

Example They <u>are not supposed to</u> / (<u>must not</u>) break the law.

1. On Sundays I <u>don't have to</u> / <u>must not</u> get up early.

2. He <u>doesn't have to</u> / <u>cannot</u> be late to work again, or else he'll lose his job.

3. Everyone enjoys the wildflowers, but people <u>shouldn't</u> / <u>don't have to</u> pick them.

4. We <u>had better not</u> / <u>cannot</u> make too much noise or we'll wake the baby.

5. You <u>may not</u> / <u>shouldn't</u> lose control of your credit card spending.

6. In most cultures, children <u>cannot</u> / <u>are not supposed to</u> correct their parents.

7. No, you <u>may not</u> / <u>shouldn't</u> stay up all night long, because you have school tomorrow.

8. She <u>is not supposed to</u> / <u>must not</u> ignore her parking ticket.

9. In some cultures, people <u>don't have to</u> / <u>cannot</u> visit other people without a gift.

■ **EXERCISE 2** Decide if the statement means *a prohibition, no permission, no obligation, advice,* or *a warning*. Write the correct explanation next to the sentence.

Example _____a warning_____ You had better not eat that fruit. You are allergic to it.

1. _a prohibition_____ You are not supposed to drive when you are very tired.

2. _No Permission,___ People cannot take books from the library without a library card.

3. _a Warning._____ You had better not call in sick to work.

4. _No obligation____ I don't have to return the money you gave me. You said it was a gift.

5. _advice_____ We shouldn't take off our coats in this cold weather.

■ **EXERCISE 3** Complete the sentence with your own ideas.

Example Teenagers had better not _____ stay out too late. _____

1. Children should not _____.

2. Teachers must not _____.

3. Tourists should not _____.

4. If you have a computer, you don't have to _____.

5. Employees must not _____.

■ **EXERCISE 4** Read the Web page and correct the mistakes. There are 6 mistakes.

Example You are not ~~suppose~~ *supposed to* swim right after you eat.

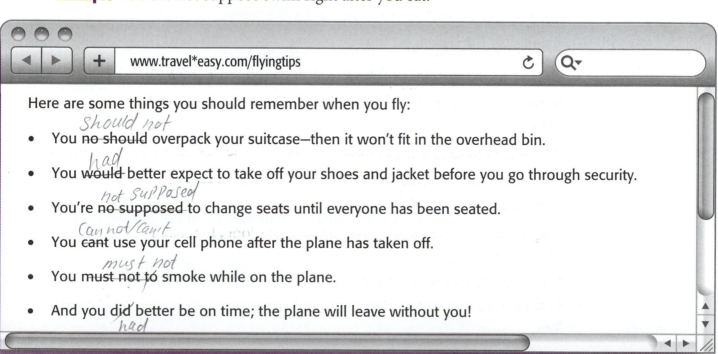

www.travel*easy.com/flyingtips

Here are some things you should remember when you fly:

• You ~~no should~~ *should not* overpack your suitcase—then it won't fit in the overhead bin.

• You ~~would~~ *had* better expect to take off your shoes and jacket before you go through security.

• You're ~~no supposed~~ *not supposed* to change seats until everyone has been seated.

• You ~~cant~~ *Can not/Can't* use your cell phone after the plane has taken off.

• You ~~must not to~~ *must not* smoke while on the plane.

• And you ~~did~~ *had* better be on time; the plane will leave without you!

Practice 44 *Will, May,* and *Might*

EXAMPLE	USE
My lease **will** expire on April 30th.	Certainty about the future
My landlord **might** raise my rent next month. I **may** move.	Possibility or uncertainty about the future
Our teacher isn't here today. She **may** be sick. / She **might** be sick.	Possibility or uncertainty about the present

■ **EXERCISE 1** (Circle) the better modal to show that the sentence is about certainty (*will*) or possibility (*may / might*).

Example My friends might / (will) come to dinner Friday at 6:30 p.m.

1. You might / (will) get a wonderful job when you graduate from college.
2. The world will / (may) become peaceful for the next 100 years.
3. Everyone (may) / will get excellent grades on the final exam.
4. She may / (will) have a hair appointment this evening.
5. We (may) / will get a little rain tonight. I can't remember what I heard.
6. I don't really know. They (might) / will move to California next year.
7. I (will) / may come to see you tomorrow morning at 9:30.
8. My first paycheck might / (will) arrive tomorrow.

■ **EXERCISE 2** Write *present* if the sentence explains a possibility about the present. Write *future* if the sentence explains a possibility about the future.

Example My cat isn't in the house. He may be hiding. ____present____

1. Their TV isn't on. Her husband may be reading. __Present__
2. The paper said that it may be warm tomorrow. __future__
3. You may have a fever. Your forehead feels hot. __Present__
4. I may find someone to tutor me in math. __futur__
5. She may go on an expensive vacation someday. __futur__

■ **EXERCISE 3** Write 3 sentences about what you *will* definitely do in the coming year. Then write 3 more about what you *may / might* do.

Examples ____I will paint my house.____   ____I may learn to grow vegetables.____

will
1. _____
2. _____
3. _____

may or *might*
1. _____
2. _____
3. _____

■ **EXERCISE 4**   Write 3 sentences about things that you definitely *won't* do in the future. Then write 3 more about things that you *may not / might not* do.

Examples   I won't buy a parrot.   I may not find a nice, cheap apartment.

won't
1. _____
2. _____
3. _____

may not or *might not*
1. _____
2. _____
3. _____

■ **EXERCISE 5**   Read the email and correct the mistakes. There are 7 mistakes.

Example On October 27th, I ~~may~~ will be a year older.

| To: | maria@bears*fan.com |
| Subject: | Baseball Game |

Hi Maria,

    Our baseball team will to play the Tigers tomorrow. Their record will may be better than ours, but we are might beat them anyway. They might to be missing a few players. I heard that the players may having the flu. It be great if we win! We might to have to go and celebrate after the game!

Your friend,

Tony

TO ASK PERMISSION	EXPLANATION
May **Could** **Can** } I write you a check?	Some English speakers consider *may* and *could* more polite than *can*.

TO ASK ANOTHER PERSON TO DO SOMETHING	EXPLANATION
Can **Will** **Could** **Would** } you plug it in?	For a request, *could* and *would* are softer than *can* and *will*.

TO EXPRESS A WANT OR DESIRE	EXPLANATION
Would you **like** to try the computer? Yes, I **would like** to see if it works. I**'d like** a glass of water.	*Would like* has the same meaning as *want*. *Would like* is more polite than *want*. The contraction for *would* after a pronoun is *'d*.

TO EXPRESS A PREFERENCE	EXPLANATION
Would you **rather** pay with cash **or** by credit card? I**'d rather** pay by credit card (**than** with cash).	We use *or* in questions with *would rather*. We use *than* in statements with *would rather*.

■ **EXERCISE 1** Circle the more polite modal.

Example (May) / Can I leave now?

1. I want / would like a cup of hot chocolate, please.
2. Will / Would you clean the kitchen after dinner?
3. Will / Could you hand me that dictionary, please?
4. I would like / want to play ball before reading the graphic novel.
5. I want / would like to see the menu, please.
6. Could / Will you get me a drink of water while you're up?
7. May / Could you look for a larger size shirt, please?
8. Dad, may / can I borrow your car tonight?
9. Would / Could I borrow your pen?
10. Would / May you help me carry the desk?

■ **EXERCISE 2** Read the description of the situation. Then write an appropriate polite request.

Example A professor asks a student to stop by her office today.

Would you stop by my office today, please?

1. A sister asks her brother to take a telephone message for her.

   Could you take a massag?

2. A police officer asks a driver to show her his driver's license.

   Would you show me your driver's license?

3. One student offers to take another student to the library.

   My I show you to the library?

4. A supervisor offers the employee either more money or more vacation time.

   Would you prefer more money or more vacation time?

5. A server offers to show a customer the dessert menu.

   Could I show you the dessert menu?

■ EXERCISE 3   Change the sentence to make it more polite.

Example Open the door.

   <u>Could you please open the door for me?</u>

1. I want to borrow your skates.

   Could I borrow your skates, Please?

2. Give me the rice.

   Could you give me the rice?

3. He wants change for a dollar.

   Could he have change for a dollar?

■ EXERCISE 4   Read the conversation and correct the mistakes. There are 10 mistakes.

Example I ~~want to~~ order dessert now.   *would like to*

Customer: ~~I can~~ cash my check?   *Can/Could I*

Bank Teller: Yes, you ~~my~~. *may.*

Customer: ~~Coud~~ you give me 5 ones and 10 tens?   *Could*

Bank Teller: Yes, I could ~~to~~.

Customer: I ~~had~~ like to pay my electric bill.   *would*

Bank Teller: Would you rather ~~to~~ pay it with cash or by check?

Customer: I ~~cans~~ pay it with cash.   *Can*

Bank Teller: Woul~~'d~~ you like me to take it out of the tens?   *would*

Customer: ~~Can?~~ *Can/Could you?*

Bank Teller: Yes, I can ~~to~~.

   Yes, I can.

SUBJECT	HAVE / HAS	PAST PARTICIPLE	COMPLEMENT
The world map	**has**	**changed**	in the past 40 years.
Some countries	**have**	**become**	independent.
She	**has**	**been**	happy to study business.

REGULAR VERBS: BASE FORM	SIMPLE PAST TENSE	PAST PARTICIPLE
study	studied	**studied**
look	looked	**looked**

IRREGULAR VERBS: BASE FORM	SIMPLE PAST TENSE	PAST PARTICIPLE
understand	understood	**understood**
come	came	**come**
run	ran	**run**
draw	drew	**drawn**
fly	flew	**flown**
know	knew	**known**
wear	wore	**worn**
break	broke	**broken**
choose	chose	**chosen**
speak	spoke	**spoken**
steal	stole	**stolen**
begin	began	**begun**
drink	drank	**drunk**
ring	rang	**rung**
swim	swam	**swum**
rise	rose	**risen**
bite	bit	**bitten**
drive	drove	**driven**
ride	rode	**ridden**
write	wrote	**written**
be	was / were	**been**
eat	ate	**eaten**
fall	fell	**fallen**
give	gave	**given**
see	saw	**seen**
make	made	**made**
take	took	**taken**
do	did	**done**
forget	forgot	**forgotten**
have / has	had	**had**
lie	lay	**lain**

EXERCISE 1 Complete the sentence with *have* or *has*.

Example I _____ *have* _____ chosen to tell you about my father.

1. He _____ *has* _____ worked as a veterinarian for 20 years.
2. My father _____ *has* _____ cured hundreds of sick dogs and cats.
3. My sister and I _____ *have* _____ helped him during school vacations.
4. We _____ *have* _____ gone with him to animal emergencies.
5. He _____ *has* _____ let me watch him work many times.

EXERCISE 2 Complete the sentence with *have* or *has* plus the past participle of the verb in parentheses.

Example I (travel / not) _____ **have not traveled** _____ to many cities in my life.

1. My friends and I (enjoy) _____ *have enjoyed* _____ visiting the museum.
2. You (begin) _____ *have begun* _____ to travel a lot in the past year.
3. My professor (take) _____ *has taken* _____ time to do more research.
4. My doctor (give) _____ *has given* _____ me a prescription for antibiotics.
5. They (start / not) _____ *have not started* _____ to jog for their health.
6. The joggers (run) _____ *have run* _____ 10 miles so far this week.
7. I (wear) _____ *has worn* _____ that blue coat only once.
8. We (not / see) _____ *have not seen* _____ that movie yet.

EXERCISE 3 Read the note and correct the mistakes. There are 8 mistakes.

Example The thieves have ~~stole~~ *stolen* my jewelry!

Over the last 50 years, Stan and I have ~~sayed~~ *seen* the world. We have ~~eated~~ *eaten* at the best restaurants and have ~~visit~~ *visited* the prettiest places. Some of the people we've met on our trips have ~~became~~ *become* our closest friends. We ~~chosen~~ *have chosen* to come back home now and have ~~began~~ *begun* to write about our adventures. So far we've ~~writed~~ *written* many pages, but Stan has ~~says~~ *said* that he wants to take another trip. We leave for Iceland tommorow. See you soon!

Past Participle. Past time that is connected to new.

Overview of the Present Perfect Tense **93**

WH–WORD	HAVE / HAS HAVEN'T / HASN'T	SUBJECT	HAVE / HAS HAVEN'T / HASN'T	PAST PARTICIPLE	COMPLEMENT	SHORT ANSWER
		I	have	been	busy.	
		I	haven't	been	available.	
	Have	you		been	tired?	Yes, I **have**. / No, I **haven't**.
Why	have	you		been	busy?	
Why	haven't	you		been	available?	
		Who	has	been	busy?	

■ EXERCISE 1   Answer the question using the present perfect tense.

Example Q: How long have you lived in this city?

A: I've lived here for only a few months.

1. **Q:** Have you ever been to Moldova?

   A: No I have never been to Moldova.

2. **Q:** How much money have you spent so far this month?

   A: _____

3. **Q:** Have you ever been on TV?

   A: _____

4. **Q:** How many movies have you seen this year?

   A: _____

5. **Q:** Have you ever gone to a movie by yourself?

   A: _____

6. **Q:** Has it rained recently?

   A: _____

7. **Q:** How many times have you moved from one house to another?

   A: _____

■ EXERCISE 2   Write a question with the words in parentheses using the present perfect tense. Answer the question about yourself.

Example (how many times / have / bad dreams)

   Q: How many times have you had bad dreams?

   A: I've had bad dreams many times.

1. (how long / have / lived in this city)

   Q: _How long have you lived in this city?_

   A: _____

2. (have / apply / for a job)

   Q: _Have you applyed for a job?_

   A: _____

3. (why / have / not / jump / out of a plane)

   Q: _Why you have not jumped out of Pane?_

   A: _____

4. (when / have / study / recently)

   Q: _When you have studied recently?_

   A: _____

5. (what / have / done / for fun / this week)

   Q: _What you have done for fun this week?_

   A: _____

6. (have / ever / make / a difficult decision)

   Q: _Have you ever made a difficult decision?_

   A: _____

■ **EXERCISE 3** **Read the email and correct the mistakes. There are 10 mistakes.**

Example I *have* been thinking of you.

To: LeeChu@my*friends.com

Subject: Job?

Dear Lee,

Why hasn't you written lately? I had missed you. I have busy at work. I have also be busy after
work. I havent' had time to finish painting the house, but I'm finished everything else. Have you
missing me? Have you hear about the job yet? The people in the office know you are available.
Have you call them? Who has you talked to? You have to write and tell me everything!

Su Lin

Practice 48 Continuation from Past to Present Tense

EXAMPLE	EXPLANATION
We **have lived** in this house **for** 10 years.	Use *for* + an amount of time: *for two years, for ten months, for a long time,* etc.
She **has been** out of town **since** Monday.	Use *since* + day, date, month, year, etc. to show when the action began: *since Tuesday, since May 2nd, since 1998,* etc.
She **has been** worried about him **since** she got the message.	Use *since* + a clause to show the start of a continuous action. The verb in the *since* clause is in the simple past tense: *since she got the message.*
How long has your brother **lived** with you?	Use *how long* to ask about the amount of time from the past to the present.
I **have always loved** to cook.	Use the present perfect tense with *always* to show that an action began in the past and continues to the present.
I **have never gone** to China.	Use the present perfect tense with *never* to show that something has not occurred from the past to the present.

Language Note: We use the present perfect tense to show that an action or state began in the past and continues to the present.

Past ————— April ——————————— Now ————→ Future

I *have had* my computer since April.

■ **EXERCISE 1** Read the paragraphs. <u>Underline</u> the present perfect verbs. (There are 15 present perfect verbs.)

Example It <u>has rained</u> for five days now.

What a flood! The water has risen, and it has covered the streets and the sidewalks. The southern parts of the town have sunk below the water. Most people who live near the river have left town. It has rained here before, but I have never seen rain like this.

The flood has been a disaster for the entire town. Everyone who has purchased a boat has been asked to bring their boats to rescue people and animals. We have swum in the water before, but now it's dirty and polluted. My family has left town. We have lived in a shelter since April 13th. Some families have been here for three weeks. I have heard of floods like this, but I have never seen one myself.

■ **EXERCISE 2** Add a time expression to each sentence.

Example (never) I have met her. <u>I have never met her.</u>

1. (for five days) She has studied for the test.

_____

Simple Present Tense versus Present Perfect Tense

SIMPLE PRESENT TENSE	PRESENT PERFECT TENSE
I **am** in the United States now.	I **have been** in the United States for two years.
She **has** a car.	She **has had** a car since November.
I **love** my job.	I **have** always **loved** my job.
He **doesn't have** a job.	He **has** never **had** a full-time job.

Language Note: The simple present tense refers only to the present time. Use the present perfect tense with *for*, *since*, *always*, or *never* to connect the past to the present time.

EXERCISE 1 Read the present tense sentence. Then use *for*, *since*, *always*, or *never* with the information in the parentheses to write a present perfect sentence that connects the past to the present time.

Example I know Maria.

(five years) <u>I have known her for five years.</u>

1. She owns a house.

(last summer) _She has owned a house last summer._

2. Eduardo lives in Chicago.

(a year and a half) _Eduardo has lived in Chicago for a year half_

3. My aunt is an excellent cook.

(always) _My aunt has al always been an excellent cook._

4. Sarah doesn't have a car.

(never) _Sarah has never have a car._

5. Gina and Tom are married.

(five years) _Gina and Tom have been married from five y_

6. He doesn't belong to the soccer club.

(never) _He has never belonged to the soccer club_

7. Allison doesn't live with her family now.

(the beginning of the year) _Allisa has not lived with her family. since_

8. She eats all her meals in the university cafeteria.

(last spring) _She has eaten all her meals in the university ca._

9. Andy and his roommate live in an apartment near campus.

(August) _Andy and his roommate have lived si since the_

10. I am a cashier at a department store.

(three years) _I have been cashier at department store for three years._

2. (never) He has lived in an apartment building.

_____ *Howlong have you lived in this city* _____

3. (since you got a job) I haven't seen you.

_____ *has* _____

4. (since Tuesday) They have waited for a letter from the lawyer.

_____

5. (since last year) You have had that coat.

_____

■ **EXERCISE 3**   **Complete the sentences about yourself, your family, or your friends present perfect tense and the time expression in parentheses.**

Example (for six months) <u>My sister hasn't seen my parents for six months.</u>

1. (since I began school)

_____

2. (for one week)

_____

3. (always)

_____

4. (since 1999)

_____

5. (for a long time)

_____

■ **EXERCISE 4**   **Read the paragraph and correct the mistakes. There are 6 mistakes.**

Example I ~~has~~ *have* never eaten Thai food.

---

www.my*life.com/my_book

have
    I never wrote anything except at school, but ~~I always have want~~ *I have always wanted* to write a book. My
has been
~~been~~ sick for several months, so I am taking care of her. I finally have some time to write.
have written   *has begun*   *am*
have write three chapters. My book have begun to take shape. I been very happy with wh

so far.

11. Gina is absent from class again today.

(she was absent last week) ~~Gina has been absent from class since~~ *last w.*

12. She wears the ring he gave her. *she has woren the ring he gave*

(they got married in 1972) ~~her since they got married in 1972~~

■ EXERCISE 2   Read the answer in the present perfect tense. Then write an appropriate question in the simple present tense.

Example Q: <u>Do you own this house?</u>

A: Yes, I've owned it since 1998.

1. Q: _____

A: Yes, he has belonged to that health club for about a year now.

2. Q: _____

A: No, I've never enjoyed exercise.

3. Q: _____

A: I've tried to, but I've never been successful.

4. Q: _____

A: No. Actually, she's never come to see us.

5. Q: _____

A: Yes. We've gone to see her several times.

■ EXERCISE 3   Read the email and correct the mistakes. There are 7 mistakes.

Example I have ~~been~~ *had* a headache for a week.

To: juanita@family*time.com

Subject: Carlos's Leg

Juanita,

Carlos ~~break~~ *broke* his leg! He has ~~have~~ *has had* a broken leg for two weeks now. He ~~have~~ *has never had* never had a broken leg before. Don't worry. Carlos' boss has ~~be~~ *has been* really nice. His boss ~~telled~~ *told* Carlos not to come back to work until his leg is better. Carlos has always ~~like~~ *has always liked* his boss. I have always ~~like~~ *liked* his boss, too.

Tony

WH– WORD	HAVE / HAS HAVEN'T / HASN'T	SUBJECT	HAVE / HAS HAVEN'T / HASN'T	BEEN	VERB + --ING	COMPLEMENT	SHORT ANSWER
		Carol	has	been	living	in the U.S.	
		She	hasn't	been	living	in Italy.	
	Has	she		been	living	in New York?	No, she **hasn't**. / Yes, she **has**.
How long	has	she		been	living	in the U.S.?	
Why	hasn't	she		been	living	in Italy?	
		Who	has	been	living	in Italy?	

Language Notes: 1. With some verbs (such as *live*, *work*, *study*, *teach*, *wear*), we can use either the present perfect tense or the present perfect continuous tense with actions that began in the past and continue into the present. There is very little difference in meaning.

2. If the action is still happening right now (at this minute), it is better to use the present perfect continuous tense.

3. Remember that we do not use the continuous form with nonaction verbs (such as *like*, *love*, *have*, *want*, *need*, *know*, *remember*, *hear*, *own*, *see*, *seem*, *understand*).

■ **EXERCISE 1** Circle the better form of the verb to complete each sentence.

Example Mother (has seemed)/ has been seeming upset since Monday.

1. How long have you watched / have you been watching this movie?
2. I have liked / been liking this city since I moved here.
3. My daughter has always loved / has always been loving to eat vegetables.
4. Why has she studied / has she been studying English since September?
5. He has worked / has been working as an engineer for many years.
6. How much have you understood / have you been understanding?
7. We have waited / have been waiting since the roast came out of the oven.
8. What have you been doing / have you done recently?

■ **EXERCISE 2** Fill in the blank with the present perfect continuous form of a verb from the box.

wait	watch	live	practice	look	~~date~~	tell	write
save	cook	exercise	expect	stay	play	read	

Examples Now that we _____ have been dating _____ for a year, I think we should get married.

How long _____ have _____ you _____ been dating _____ Joe?

1. The soup _____ for two hours. I think it's ready.

2. How long _____ she _____?
   If her friend doesn't arrive soon, she'll give up.

3. He _____ everywhere for his keys, but he can't find them.

4. Why _____ I _____ for two hours?
   My muscles are going to be sore tomorrow!

5. You _____ TV all evening. Shouldn't you stop and do
   your homework?

6. Renée _____ in Montreal, but she's moving to Toronto
   next month.

7. Come in. We _____ you.

8. I _____ this book for hours. My eyes are getting tired.

9. _____ you _____ the piano lately?

10. She _____ her money, and now she's ready to buy a new
    computer.

■ **EXERCISE 3**   **Read the Web page and correct the mistakes. There are 9 mistakes.**

Example I ^ been studying English for six months.
have

www.polarbear*extinction.com

Polar Bears and Global Warming

Recent News

If you been watching the news lately, you have be hearing that polar bears are in danger

of extinction.

Fact or Fiction?

Some scientists have been said that the polar ice is melting. They has been blaming

global warming for the melting. Polar bears have been lived on polar ice for hundreds of years.

If the ice melts, the polar bears cannot live.

Other scientists had been arguing that global warming does not exist. They also say that

the ice are melting at the same speed it has always been melt. They claim that the polar bears

have dying off at the same rate as they did in earlier years.

Practice 51 Present Perfect Tense with Indefinite Time in the Past

EXAMPLE	EXPLANATION
Have you **ever gone** to a family reunion? Yes, I**'ve gone** to many family reunions. **Have** you **ever used** a search engine? Yes, I **have**. / No, I **haven't**. **Has** Carol **ever gone** to Thailand? No, she **never has**.	A question with *ever* asks about any time between the past and the present. Put *ever* between the subject and the past participle. We can answer an *ever* question with a frequency response: *a few times, many times, often, never,* etc.
Has Carol **met** her cousin **yet**? Yes, she **has already met** her cousin. **Have** you **cleaned** your room **yet**? No, I **haven't cleaned** it **yet**. / No, **not yet**.	*Yet* and *already* refer to an indefinite time in the near past. Use *yet* in questions and negatives. Use *already* in affirmative statements.
Have you **washed** the dishes **yet**? Yes, I **have just washed** them.	*Just* shows that something happened very recently.

Language Note: We use the present perfect tense to refer to an action that occurred at an indefinite time in the past and still has importance to the present situation.

```
                                          Now
Past ———|——————————?——————————|————————————→ Future
        Have you ever used a
        search engine?
```

■ **EXERCISE 1** Fill in each blank with *ever, already, yet,* or *just*. In some cases, more than one of the words can be used.

Example Haven't you finished _____ yet? _____

1. You're too late. The doctor has _____ just _____ left for the day.
2. Have you _____ ever _____ ridden a horse? It's fun!
3. I've _____ already _____ invited him to my party.
4. I'm so tired of that book! I've _____ already _____ read it three times.
5. Why haven't you written him _____ yet _____?
6. Have you _____ ever _____ felt lonely?
7. Don't touch the dresser! I've _____ painted it.
8. I've _____ seen Hernando; he looks upset.
9. She hasn't contacted us _____, but I'm sure she will soon.
10. I haven't told her about my plans _____.
11. Have you _____ read a graphic novel?
12. We have to wait because their plane hasn't arrived _____.

■ EXERCISE 2   Unscramble the words to write a correct statement or question.

Example found / new / I / already / roommate / a / have

I have already found a new roommate.

1. the door / my roommate / just / in / come / has

   My roommate has just come in the door.

2. ever / the oil / this car / checked / haven't / you / in

   Have you ever checked the oil in this car?

3. she / to / already / three universities / applied / has

   She has already to applead three universties.

4. the meat / anyone / the refrigerator / why / in / put / hasn't / yet

   Why hasn't anyone put the meat in the refrigerator yet?

5. just / their landlord / has / them / to move / asked

   Their landlord has just asked them to move.

6. had / bad news / you / your family / have / to / ever / to break

   Have you ever had to break bad news to your family.

7. the checkbook / balanced / yet / haven't / I

   I haven't balanced the checkbook yet.

8. seen / have / we / movie / already / that / romantic

   We have already seen that romantic movie.

■ EXERCISE 3   Read the conversation and correct the mistakes. There are 8 mistakes.

Example Has your friend ever ~~make~~ *made* you dinner?

Anya: Have you ever ~~visit~~ *visited* the Grand Canyon?

Keelia: No, I ~~ever~~ *never* have.

Anya: Has anyone in your family ~~never~~ *ever* been to the Grand Canyon?

Keelia: Sophie went there. She had fun.

Anya: I have just ~~make~~ *I've* plans to go. I already buy my ticket.

Keelia: I'm often thought about going.

Anya: Have you ever ~~talk~~ *talked* to your husband about it?

Keelia: No, I ~~ever~~ *never* have. But I would like to go.

Anya: You should go soon. You will have fun!

Practice 52 Overview of Gerunds

EXAMPLES	USE OF GERUND
Camping is a popular outdoor activity.	A gerund can be the subject. It takes a singular verb.
Many people enjoy **swimming**. I miss **seeing** you in class. They avoid **studying** on Saturday nights.	A gerund can be the object. Some verbs (such as *enjoy, miss, avoid, quit, suggest*) are followed by a gerund.
Some people are in favor **of hunting**, but others are opposed to it. I'm **interested in learning** more about computers.	A gerund can be the object of a preposition. Some adjectives are followed by a preposition + gerund.
Today you can buy your clothes **by shopping** on the Internet. You should practice **by studying** interview questions.	A gerund can be part of an adverbial phrase. Some verbs are followed by a preposition + gerund.
I like to **go shopping**.	Special (idiomatic) expressions with *go* use a gerund: *go dancing, go swimming, go fishing, go shopping.*

Language Notes:
1. A gerund phrase is a gerund + a noun: *finding a job, learning English.*
2. We can put *not* in front of a gerund (phrase) to make it negative:
   Not having a job is frustrating.
3. These verbs can be followed by a gerund:

admit	*discuss*	*mind*	*put off*
appreciate	*dislike*	*miss*	*quit*
avoid	*enjoy*	*permit*	*recommend*
can't help	*finish*	*postpone*	*risk*
consider	*keep*	*practice*	*suggest*

■ **EXERCISE 1** Fill in each blank with the gerund form of one of the verbs in the box.

climb	wash	camp	~~smoke~~	practice	study
do	sail	think	help	exercise	listen

Example _____Smoking_____ is not allowed on airplanes.

1. ____listening____ to music is a good way to relax.
2. ____studying____ all night before a test can make you tired.
3. I bought a special rope for mountain ____climbing____.
4. There's a good breeze today. Let's go ____sailing____.
5. I am trying to lose weight by ____exercising____ regularly.
6. I know you want to avoid ____washing____ the dishes.

7. Even during an exam she can't help ___*thinking*___ about her grades.

8. He improved his performance by ___*Practicing*___ over and over.

9. You shouldn't delay ___*doing*___ the things that need to be done.

10. ___*Helping*___ patients to get well is a nurse's job.

■ **EXERCISE 2** **Answer the question about you with a sentence that contains a gerund.**

Example **Q:** What makes you tired?

A: ___Studying all night___ makes me tired.

1. **Q:** When do you shop for groceries?

   A: I go _____.

2. **Q:** What do you really enjoy doing?

   A: I really enjoy _____.

3. **Q:** How do you quit a bad habit?

   A: I quit by _____.

4. **Q:** What don't you like doing?

   A: I dislike _____.

5. **Q:** What do you think is boring?

   A: I consider _____.

■ **EXERCISE 3** **Read the conversation and correct the mistakes. There are 8 mistakes.**

Example I think ~~play~~ *playing* baseball is really good for you.

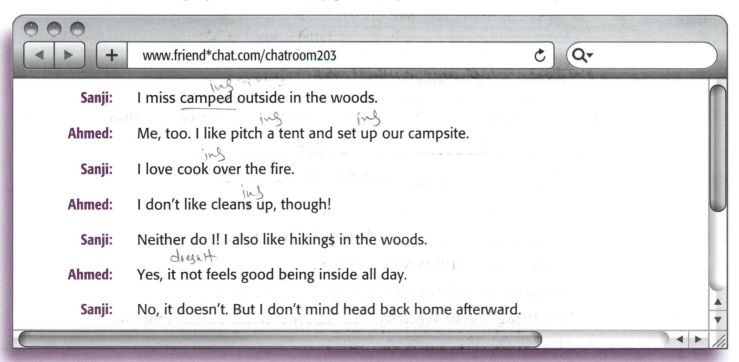

Sanji: I miss camped *ing* outside in the woods.

Ahmed: Me, too. I like pitch *ing* a tent and set *ing* up our campsite.

Sanji: I love cook *ing* over the fire.

Ahmed: I don't like cleans *ing* up, though!

Sanji: Neither do I! I also like hikings in the woods.

Ahmed: Yes, it *doesn't* not feels good being inside all day.

Sanji: No, it doesn't. But I don't mind head back home afterward.

Practice 53 Overview of Infinitives

EXAMPLE	EXPLANATION
I want **to find** a job.	An infinitive is used after certain verbs.
I want you **to help**.	An object can be added before an infinitive.
I'm happy **to help** you.	An infinitive can follow certain adjectives.
It's important **to have** a good résumé.	An infinitive follows certain expressions with *it*.
He went to a counselor **to get** advice.	An infinitive is used to show purpose.

■ **EXERCISE 1** Fill in each blank with the infinitive form of a verb from the box.

Example It's going to take more money _____ to pay _____ for your purchases.

~~pay~~	understand	travel	stay	drive
give	swim	eat	operate	tell
earn	win	call	speak	communicate

1. My parents didn't want me _____ to travel _____ to another country alone.
2. In some countries it's illegal _____ to drive _____ a car without insurance.
3. Many people today use email _____ to communicate _____ with each other.
4. Her parents made her promise not _____ to stay _____ out late.
5. They forgot _____ to tell _____ us what time they would arrive.
6. It can be dangerous _____ to swim _____ in the ocean.
7. His pronunciation is a little bit hard _____ to understand _____.
8. Many parents tell their children not _____ to speak _____ to strangers.
9. Patients can just push this button _____ to call _____ a nurse.
10. Cars with big engines are more expensive _____ to operate/drive _____.
11. The robbers forced the man _____ to give _____ them all his money.
12. You were really lucky _____ to win _____ that contest.

■ **EXERCISE 2** Unscramble the words to write a correct statement.

Example my vocabulary words / to write / like / in a notebook / I

I like to write my vocabulary words in a notebook.

1. to write / my compositions / a computer / use / I

   I use a computer to write my compositions

2. easy / the application forms / it / to complete / wasn't

   It wasn't easy to complete the application form.

3. me / a souvenir / your brother / to bring / wants / him / from our trip

   Your brother wants me to bring him from our trip

4. is / handwriting / to read / my / hard

   My handwriting is hard to read.

5. expect / my money / my parents / carefully / me / to spend

   My Parents expect me to spend my money carefully.

■ **EXERCISE 3   Answer the question with a complete sentence that contains an infinitive.**

Example What takes a long time to learn? <u>It takes a long time to learn to cook well.</u>

1. **Q:** What's an important thing that your family has asked you to do?

   A: _____

2. **Q:** What are children too young to do safely?

   A: _____

3. **Q:** What is important to do every day?

   A: _____

4. **Q:** What do you need to do today?

   A: _____

■ **EXERCISE 4   Read the email and correct the mistakes. There are 10 mistakes.**

Example Dolphins like ‸to play in the water.

To: UncleChan235@home*town.com

Subject: Thank You!

Dear Uncle,

   My teacher said that I have to work harder. So I plan to study every night when I get home. I want to succeed succeeding in school. I want to find a good job when I finish. I want to speak speaking English better and to write wrote what is in my heart. I would like people to listening to what I have to say. But for now, I want to thanking you for helping me get this far. I would like to returning your kindness by working for you this summer.

Your nephew,

Sung-hoon

EXAMPLE	EXPLANATION
To learn another language takes a long time. **It**'s fun **to practice** with my classmates.	An infinitive can be used as the subject of a sentence. We can also begin the sentence with *it* and delay the infinitive.
It is easy **for children to learn** another language. **It**'s difficult **for adults to learn** another language.	Include *for* + noun / object pronoun to make a statement that is true for a specific person or group.

Language Notes: 1. When we use an infinitive after these adjectives, the first word in the sentence is usually *it*:

dangerous	*good*	*necessary*
difficult	*great*	*possible*
easy	*hard*	*sad*
expensive	*important*	*wrong*
fun	*impossible*	

2. There is no difference in meaning between an infinitive subject and a gerund subject.
It's important *to arrive on time.*   *Arriving on time* is important.

■ EXERCISE 1   Complete the sentence with an infinitive phrase.

Example It isn't healthy <u>to eat a lot of greasy foods.</u>

1. It is impossible _____.

2. It's frightening _____.

3. It's very relaxing _____.

4. It's sad _____.

5. It is wrong _____.

6. It is important _____.

7. It is foolish _____.

8. It's illegal _____.

■ EXERCISE 2   Rewrite the sentence using an infinitive. Do not change the meaning of the sentence.

Example Rollerskating takes a good sense of balance.

<u>It takes a good sense of balance to rollerskate.</u>

1. Correcting your own bad habits is not easy.

_____

2. Understanding other cultures is sometimes difficult.

_____

3. Getting to the concert early was smart.

_____

4. Waking up in a tent in the mountains is a great feeling.

_____

5. Getting a master's degree will take me two more years.

_____

6. Watching television all day is pretty boring.

_____

7. Seeing people go hungry is very sad.

_____

8. Is copying my roommate's homework wrong?

_____

■ **EXERCISE 3** **Change the gerund subject to an infinitive subject.**

Example Renting a car is expensive. _It's expensive to rent a car._

1. Driving at night is dangerous.

_____

2. Going to school without a computer is difficult.

_____

3. Staying at home on Saturday night isn't fun.

_____

■ **EXERCISE 4** **Read the paragraph and correct the mistakes. There are 8 mistakes.**

Example ~~Is~~ It is expensive to go on vacation.

It's fun ~~make~~ to make pasta. It takes a little time to ~~cooking~~ to cook, but it is not difficult. The first thing you need

to do is fill a pot with water and put it on the stove. It will take a few minutes for the water ~~boiling~~ to boil. When the

water boils, add the pasta. It will take about 10 minutes for the pasta to ~~cooking~~ to cook. It is important ~~stirring~~ to stir

the pasta. If you don't stir it, the pasta will stick together. When the pasta is chewy but not hard, it is

time to ~~taking~~ to take the pot off the stove and ~~draining~~ to drain the water. Then add some sauce and enjoy!

Practice 55 Infinitives after Adjectives

EXAMPLE	EXPLANATION
I'm **embarrassed to go** to the party in these old clothes. He was **surprised to get** a call from his teacher.	Some adjectives can be followed by an infinitive.

Language Note: Some adjectives are often followed by an infinitive:

afraid	glad	relieved
ashamed	happy	sad
disappointed	lucky	sorry
embarrassed	proud	surprised
	ready	upset

■ **EXERCISE 1**   (Circle) the underlined word(s) to complete the sentence.

Example Are you (ready) / proud to leave for the airport?

1. He (was sorry) / was glad to see his low grade on the exam.

2. They were embarrassed / (were upset) to hear about their friend's accident.

3. Some people is afraid / (are afraid) to go outside after dark.

4. She (was happy) / was disappointed to learn that it wasn't going to cost much.

5. We were upset / (lucky) to get a taxi while it was raining.

6. It was no trouble at all. We are afraid / (are glad) to help you.

7. They are ashamed / (lucky) to find a nice house and a reliable car.

8. You should be proud / (ashamed) to waste all that food.

9. They were sorry / (proud) to watch their daughter win the race.

10. She was upset / (relieved) to hear that her baby was healthy.

11. My family was (ready) / sad to leave on vacation.

12. Our neighbors were (proud) / ashamed to show us their beautiful flower garden.

13. The police were (ready) / upset to help people in a car accident.

14. The teenagers were disappointed / (embarrassed) to receive kisses from their mother.

15. His sister was ready / (afraid) to walk home alone at night.

■ **EXERCISE 2**   Complete each sentence with an infinitive.

Example Parents are sad _to see their children suffer._

1. Parents are proud _____.

2. Students are lucky _____.

3. Mice are afraid _____.

4. Dogs are happy _____.

5. Climbers are relieved _____.

6. Teenagers are eager _____.

7. I will be glad _____.

8. I am very embarrassed _____.

9. My cousin is ready _____.

10. I will be sorry _____.

11. My friend was upset _____.

12. Our neighbors were prepared _____.

■ **EXERCISE 3** **Fill in each blank with a subject + an appropriate form of the verb _be_.**

Examples _____*She was*_____ ashamed to receive poor grades.

_____*I am*_____ sorry to hear that you are sick.

1. _____ lucky to have so many wonderful friends.

2. _____ scared to drive her car in a snowstorm last night.

3. _____ afraid to speak on the telephone.

4. _____ surprised to receive my letter yesterday.

5. _____ glad to meet you at the party last week.

■ **EXERCISE 4** **Read the email and correct the mistakes. There are 8 mistakes.**

Example Marta will be disappointed ^to^ know you won't be there.

To: papi@my*family.com

Subject: Michelle

Dear Papi,

I am unhappy ^to^ tell you that Michelle was in an accident. But I am relieved ^to^ tell you that she is

going to be fine. She is lucky ^to^ be alive. She was on her bicycle and was hit by a car. She is ashamed ^to^ talk

to you and sorry ^to^ cause you to worry. I think she is embarrassed ^to^ admit that it was partly her fault. She

was not watching where she was going. She will be ready ^to^ come home this afternoon. I know you

will be happy ^to^ see her.

Your son,

Antoine

Practice 56 Infinitives after Verbs

EXAMPLE	EXPLANATION
Both sides agreed **to end** the war. Some of the soldiers refused **to go** home. People began **to rebuild** their homes. Everyone decided **to make** a new start.	Some verbs are commonly followed by an infinitive or infinitive phrase.

Language Note: We can use an infinitive or infinitive phrase after the following verbs:

agree	forget	prefer
ask	hope	promise
attempt	learn	refuse
begin	like	remember
continue	love	start
decide	need	try
expect	plan	want

■ EXERCISE 1 Fill in each blank with the infinitive form of a verb from the box.

Example The soldiers tried _____to invade_____ the city, but they couldn't.

~~invade~~	receive	wait	help	be	destroy
work	send	lose	resist	give	

1. No one expected the city ____to be____ able to resist their attack.
2. The enemy forgot ____to destroy____ the main bridge across the river.
3. The government asked other countries ____to help____.
4. The other countries preferred ____to wait____ and see what happened.
5. The people didn't want ____to lose____ their homes to the enemy.
6. They learned ____to work____ together for the common good.
7. They continued ____to resist____ the enemy month after month.
8. They needed ____to receive____ fresh supplies of food and arms.

■ EXERCISE 2 Fill in each blank with the appropriate verb. The verbs in the box may be used more than once. Use the correct verb tense.

Example At the wedding last week, the bride and groom ____promised____ to love each other.

decide	hope	prefer	need
continue	refuse	like	begin
ask	promise	want	start

1. After much discussion, we _____decided_____ to talk about the pollution problem.

2. It _____ to rain day after day after day.

3. My parents _____ to retire while they are still healthy and active.

4. The policeman _____ to see the woman's driver's license.

5. She _____ to show it to him.

6. You _____ to tell me what kind of flowers you wanted me to buy.

■ **EXERCISE 3**   **Write an appropriate answer to the question using an infinitive.**

Example What was your plan for your future when you were a child?

<u>I planned to be an astronaut when I grew up.</u>

1. What activity do you love to do?

_____

2. What do you need to do this week?

_____

3. What have you tried unsuccessfully to do?

_____

4. What interesting thing have you begun in the past six months?

_____

■ **EXERCISE 4**   **Read the paragraph and correct the mistakes. There are 8 mistakes.**

Example I hope ˄to find work as an interpreter one day.

I remember when my brother decided ˄to tie his shoes while he was walking down the stairs. He had just learned ˄to tie his shoes. We were playing outside. He want~~ed to~~ go inside for a minute. When he was inside, his laces became untied. He started ˄to come back outside. He wanted ˄to save time, so he bent over ˄to grab his shoelaces. He fell over and began ˄to fall down the stairs. I caught him at the bottom of the stairs. He promised never ˄to do that again!

Practice 57　Gerunds or Infinitives after Verbs

GERUND	INFINITIVE
I started **looking** for a job a month ago. He continued **working** until he was 68.	I started **to look** for a job a month ago. He continued **to work** until he was 68.

Some verbs can be followed by either a gerund or an infinitive:		
attempt	deserve	prefer
begin	hate	start
can't stand	like	try
continue	love	

Language Note:　*Try* followed by a gerund is a little different from *try* followed by an infinitive:
- Gerund: If you can't find a job, you should try *networking*. [*try* = use a different technique]
- Infinitive: I'll try *to improve* my résumé. [*try* = make an effort]

■ **EXERCISE 1**　**Change the infinitive to a gerund or the gerund to an infinitive. Pay attention to verb tenses.**

Example　I started working at the fast-food restaurant last week.

　　　　　I started to work at the fast-food restaurant last week.

1. All children deserve someone looking after them.

　　_____

2. I prefer swimming in lakes.

　　_____

3. She began to work at the grocery store when she was 16 years old.

　　_____

4. We hate worrying about our children's safety.

　　_____

5. Our parents started to form a group to talk to the teachers.

　　_____

6. You can't stand eating red meat.

　　_____

7. I liked talking to my friends every day after school.

　　_____

8. The man tried to help people who were lost.

　　_____

9. The women continue to volunteer for the library.

_____

10. We love visiting our aunt and uncle.

_____

11. They deserved winning the writing prize.

_____

12. It begins getting colder this time of year.

_____

■ EXERCISE 2 **Fill in each blank with the infinitive or gerund form of the verb in parentheses.**

Example I wish you would remember (infinitive: take) _____**to take**_____ off your shoes before you come into the house.

1. Try (gerund: learn) _____ at least 10 new vocabulary words every day.

2. People who have trouble falling asleep should try (gerund: read) _____ in bed.

3. We tried (infinitive: push) _____ the car out of the road, but it was stuck.

4. The plants will die if you don't start (infinitive: water) _____ them.

5. I love (infinitive: walk) _____ in the woods in the fall.

■ EXERCISE 3 **Read the paragraph and correct the mistakes. There are 8 mistakes.**

Example I hated to ~~driving~~ _drive_ when I first got my license.

Did you watch the Olympics? I love to watching the ice skaters. As they begin spin around and _[to watch/watching]_ _[to spin/spining]_

around, they continuing to stay in one place. It seems like they are trying cut a hole in the ice. I prefer _[continue]_ _[to cut]_

watch the ice dancers, however. They are so graceful. When they attempt to throwing their partners into _[to]_ _[to throw]_

the air, I can't stand think that one would fall and get hurt. They rarely do. I think they all deserve getting a _[to to think/thinking]_ _[to get]_

medal!

Practice 58 Infinitives to Show Purpose

EXAMPLE	EXPLANATION
You can use the Internet **to find** information about jobs. He's saving his money **to buy** a house.	We use the infinitive to show the purpose of an action. We can also say *in order to*: I am studying *in order to* get a good grade.

■ EXERCISE 1   Unscramble the words to write a correct statement or question.

Example to pay / to sell / I / my plane ticket / had / for / my textbooks / in order

I had to sell my textbooks in order to pay for my plane ticket.

1. in the newspaper / she / a new roommate / an ad / to find / put

   _____

2. had / here / to take / we / three buses / to get / in order

   _____

3. weight / in order / should / what / do / to lose / I

   _____

4. these / your arms / to strengthen / you / should / do / exercises

   _____

5. with your teacher / an appointment / to review / make / your test

   _____

6. 10 words / to build / every day / you / can / your vocabulary / in order / learn

   _____

■ EXERCISE 2   Complete the sentence with an infinitive to show purpose. Choose an infinitive from the box for your answer.

Example People use a dictionary to look up words they don't know.

to dispose of	to keep	to cut	to buy	to write
to clean	to buy	to call	to research	to find
to look up	to cool off	to show	to pay for	

1. People use a refrigerator _____.

2. People use money _____.

3. Travelers use passports _____.

4. People use cell phones _____.

5. Students use computers _____.

6. Travelers use maps _____.

7. Shoppers use credit cards _____.

8. People use libraries _____.

9. People use trash cans _____.

10. People use air conditioners _____.

■ **EXERCISE 3**   **Answer the questions about yourself.**

Example What do you listen to music for?

<u>I listen to classical music in order to relax.</u>

1. What do you do in order to relax?

_____

2. What will you use your education for?

_____

■ **EXERCISE 4**   **Read the Web page and correct the mistakes. There are 5 mistakes.**

Example You can save your money in order ^to^ buy what you want.

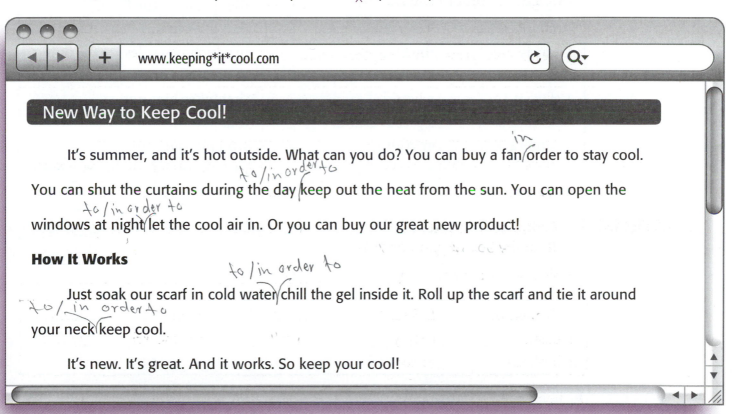

New Way to Keep Cool!

It's summer, and it's hot outside. What can you do? You can buy a fan ~~in~~/order to stay cool. You can shut the curtains during the day *to/in order to* keep out the heat from the sun. You can open the windows at night *to/in order to* let the cool air in. Or you can buy our great new product!

How It Works

Just soak our scarf in cold water *to/in order to* chill the gel inside it. Roll up the scarf and tie it around your neck *to/in order to* keep cool.

It's new. It's great. And it works. So keep your cool!

EXAMPLE	EXPLANATION
Marlene would like to marry someone **who knows how to cook**. Rafael would like to have a job **that / which uses his talents**. The man **who(m) you married** is very responsible. The job **that / which I have** gives me a lot of satisfaction.	An adjective clause is a group of words that describes a noun. It follows the noun. Relative pronouns introduce an adjective clause: *who(m)* for people, *which* for things, *that* for people and things.

■ EXERCISE 1   Match the phrases to make 9 logical definitions.

Example Breakfast is the meal that people eat in the morning.

~~Breakfast is~~	a situation	that fall from the sky.
Ink is	people	who has to work for no pay.
A rug is	a dessert	that protects the floor.
Firefighters are	ice crystals	that goes in our pens.
A war is	~~the meal~~	in which two sides are in conflict.
Trash is	a piece of equipment	that children love.
A slave is	a liquid	that takes pictures.
Ice cream is	a piece of cloth	that people throw away.
A camera is	anything	who put out fires.
Snow is	a person	~~that people eat in the morning.~~

1. _____
2. _____
3. _____
4. _____
5. _____
6. _____
7. _____
8. _____
9. _____

■ EXERCISE 2   Fill in each blank with *who, that,* or *which*.

Example This is the story of a man _____who_____ lost a key.

1. The maid _____ found the key was cleaning the room.
2. The key _____ she found had some words on it.

3. The maid threw the key _____ she found into the garbage can.

4. The trash collector _____ worked at the hotel read the words on the key.

5. The trash collector _____ was curious put the key in a bag.

6. The trash collector took the key to a shopkeeper _____ worked next door.

7. The shopkeeper _____ thanked the man identified the key.

8. The shopkeeper paid $100 to the trash collector _____ found the key in the garbage can.

9. The shopkeeper used the key _____ opened a safe.

10. It opened a safe _____ contained many diamond rings.

■ **EXERCISE 3**   Underline the adjective clause. Circle the noun described by the adjective clause.

Example   I enjoy movies that have happy endings.

1. I like people who have nice smiles.

2. He enjoys music that helps him relax.

3. We like to relax in places that are peaceful.

4. They want to know college students who like to travel.

5. She chose the black skirt that makes her look thin.

6. You look at magazines that are about world news.

■ **EXERCISE 4**   Read the conversation and correct the mistakes. There are 6 mistakes.

Example   The song is about a dog ~~who~~ *that* rescues her owner.

Sasha: I like to watch movies who tell a story. Do you?

Berta: Yes. I like watching those movies. The characters are the people which tell the story.

Sasha: I like a story who makes me think.

Berta: Who decides which lines the actors speak?

Sasha: I think it's the writer decides that.

Berta: Is there a story what you'd like to tell?

Sasha: I'd like to write a story in who everyone is happy.

Practice 60 Relative Pronouns as Subjects

A relative pronoun can be the subject of the adjective clause.

He wants to meet a woman. A woman likes sports.

He wants to meet a woman | who / that | likes sports.

An advertisement   is expensive to create.

An advertisement has a lot of words.

An advertisement | that / which | has a lot of words is expensive to create.

Language Notes: 1. In informal English, we can use *that* for both things and people.
2. In the present tense, the verb of the adjective clause must agree with the preceding noun (singular/plural):
An advertisement that *has* a lot of words can be expensive.
Advertisements that *have* a lot of words can be expensive.
3. *Who* and *that* in an adjective clause can contract with *is*:
He's looking for someone *who's* smarter than he is.

■ EXERCISE 1 Circle the correct form of the verb in the adjective clause.

Example I know a girl who (comes)/ come from Somalia.

1. What's the name of the person who <u>is / are</u> singing that song?
2. He wants to marry someone who <u>understand / understands</u> him.
3. We welcome everyone who <u>come / comes</u> to learn.
4. She'll have to borrow the money that <u>is / are</u> needed.
5. Will the person who <u>has / have</u> my notebook please return it?
6. You ate the rest of the cookies that <u>was / were</u> in the box.
7. The lady who <u>work / works</u> at the cash register will give you a receipt.
8. Could you bring us some of the apples that <u>grow / grows</u> on your apple tree?
9. I bought pens that <u>don't / doesn't</u> write well.
10. I really don't like sports that <u>is / are</u> violent.

■ EXERCISE 2 Unscramble the words to make a correct statement or question with an adjective clause.

Example love / I / kind to me / the aunt / was / who

<u>I love the aunt who was kind to me.</u>

1. the man / to play / taught / that's / the flute / who / me

   _____

2. which / the car / was / bought / old and ugly / we

   _____

3. painted / who / who / that painting / the artist / was

   _____

4. get / are / people / upset / very sensitive / easily / who / there

   _____

5. today / this / came / is / the mail / that

   _____

6. which / we / on the first / must / pay / of the month / are due / the bills

   _____

7. a friend / have / you / can help / do / who / me

   _____

8. that / the most options / the computer / prefer / has / I

   _____

9. dropped / where / who / is / this wallet / the person

   _____

10. buy / works / let's / better / than this one / an umbrella / that

    _____

■ **EXERCISE 3   Read the paragraph and correct the mistakes. There are 7 mistakes.**

Example My sweater that ~~have~~ _has_ a hole in it is on the table.

> ### Antonia's New Job
>
> Antonia got a job at a company that have an office downtown. Every morning, she takes the bus
>
> that left the station at 7:45. When she gets to her job, she has to check in with her boss. Her boss has
>
> a schedule that tell everyone what to do that day. Her boss is a man which comes from the same town
>
> that she come from. Many of her coworkers are people who comes from other countries. Some of them
>
> have accents that is hard to understand, but she tries her best.

Practice 61 Relative Pronouns as Objects

A relative pronoun can be the object of the adjective clause.

He discussed the hobbies. He has <u>hobbies</u>.

He discussed the hobbies | **that** / **which** / **ø** | he has.

The woman   likes sports.

He met the <u>woman</u>.

The woman | **who(m)** / **that** / **ø** | he met likes sports.

Language Note: The correct object form of the relative pronoun for people is *whom.* However, in conversation, *who* is often heard. Or the relative pronoun is omitted completely:
Formal: The woman *whom* he met likes sports.
Informal: The woman *who* he met likes sports.
Informal: The woman he met likes sports.

■ **EXERCISE 1**   Fill in the blank with *who, whom,* or *which.* (Do not use *that.*)

Example The politician _____ <u>who / whom</u> _____ we met yesterday was very friendly.

1. I got tickets to the concert _____ you told us about.

2. The movie _____ we saw yesterday was very exciting.

3. There is the man _____ I'm going to marry.

4. The envelope _____ you sent me was empty.

5. The woman _____ you spoke to was my mother's cousin.

6. I liked the book _____ you gave me for my birthday.

7. I have several friends _____ like to get together whenever possible.

8. My doctor told me to avoid foods _____ have lots of sugar.

9. I like a man _____ knows what he wants.

10. The food _____ we ate was very spicy.

■ **EXERCISE 2**   <u>Underline</u> the adjective clause in the sentence. Then ~~cross out~~ the relative pronoun to make the sentence or question informal. Rewrite the sentence with no relative pronoun.

Example Did you read all the books ~~that~~ <u>the teacher assigned</u>?

Informal: <u>Did you read all the books the teacher assigned?</u>

1. I like the people that I met at your house yesterday.

Informal: _____

2. This is the man whom I spoke of last week.

Informal: _____

3. The reason that you gave was not good enough.

Informal: _____

4. Spring is the season that I like best.

Informal: _____

5. The teacher that I wanted to speak to was on vacation.

Informal: _____

6. What did you say to the girl whom I met yesterday?

Informal: _____

7. The music that they played was too loud.

Informal: _____

8. I waited all day for the repairman that you recommended.

Informal: _____

9. The soccer games that we played in high school were always exciting.

Informal: _____

10. I enjoyed reading the book that you recommended.

Informal: _____

11. He got that camera from the woman whom I told you about.

Informal: _____

■ **EXERCISE 3   Read the paragraph and correct the mistakes. There are 6 mistakes.**

Example The author wrote a book for people ~~which~~ who need help with computers.

I had a great time at my reunion! I saw people that I haven't seen in many years. The first person

which I saw was Fatima. She is a classmate whose I've known since I came here. Then I saw Boris. He is the

guy which I sat behind in English class. He lives in Miami now and said that I should visit him there. Next

I saw Mr. Rosenberg. He is the history teacher which everyone loved. I also saw Mia. She's the person which

I miss the most. She moved to Australia. Seeing them reminded me how much I liked high school.

Practice 62 Comparative and Superlative Forms

	SIMPLE	COMPARATIVE	SUPERLATIVE
One-syllable adjectives and adverbs	tall	**taller**	**the tallest**
Two-syllable adjectives that end in –y	easy	**easier**	**the easiest**
Other two-syllable adjectives	frequent	**more frequent**	**the most frequent**
Some two-syllable adjectives have two forms: *simple, common, handsome, quiet, gentle, narrow, clever, friendly, angry.*	simple	**simpler** **more simple**	**the simplest** **the most simple**
Adjectives with three or more syllables	important	**more important**	**the most important**
–ly adverbs	quickly	**more quickly**	**the most quickly**
Irregular adjectives and adverbs	good / well bad / badly little a lot far	**better** **worse** **less** **more** **farther / further**	**the best** **the worst** **the least** **the most** **the farthest / furthest**

Language Notes: 1. Most adjectives that end in –ed and –ing use *more* and *the most* (not –er or –est):
more tired   *the most* disturbing
2. The comparative form compares two similar things, and uses *than*. The superlative form compares one thing to two or more other similar things:
Comparative: The blue car is *faster than* the red car.
Superlative: That ring is *the most beautiful* of those five rings.
3. *Farther* is used for distances; *further* is used for ideas.

■ EXERCISE 1   Circle the correct form of the adjective.

Example That is the <u>more ugly</u> / (ugliest) dog that I have ever seen.

1. This has been the <u>wonderfulest / most wonderful</u> birthday party of my life.

2. I ate two sandwiches, but Akim was <u>hungrier / more hungry</u> and ate three.

3. Those were the <u>deliciousest / most delicious</u> sandwiches I've ever eaten.

4. Don't be so rude. Try to ask <u>politer / more politer</u> questions.

5. Isis is too nervous for this job. We need someone <u>calmer / more calm</u>.

6. You're the <u>interestingest / most interesting</u> person I've met at school.

7. Hawaii is a much <u>wetter / more wet</u> place than Arizona.

8. As she grew older, she became <u>beautifuller / more beautiful</u>.

9. You need to get to the store <u>earlier / more early</u> if you want to find the best bargains.

10. No <u>farther / further</u> meetings have been scheduled.

11. I'm sorry, I don't understand. Could you repeat that <u>slowlier / more slowly</u>?

■ **EXERCISE 2** (Circle) the correct simple, comparative, or superlative form.

Example This test is <u>important / more important /</u> (<u>the most important</u>) of all the tests.

1. That was a very <u>rough / rougher / roughest</u> airplane flight.

2. She's <u>good / better / the best</u> than most of her classmates in math.

3. I'm afraid that I did really <u>badly / worse / the worst</u> on that exam.

4. Many Americans think that Abraham Lincoln was the <u>great / greater / greatest</u> American president.

5. This new clock radio is absolutely <u>useless / more useless / the most useless</u>.

6. The <u>hot / hotter / hottest</u> place in the world is in Mauritania.

7. Every night you come home <u>late / later / the latest</u> than the night before.

8. Is it true that Athens is the <u>noisy / noisier / noisiest</u> city in the world?

9. Some people are <u>friendly / friendlier / the friendliest</u> than others.

10. I want to buy a <u>pretty / prettier / the prettiest</u> dress.

■ **EXERCISE 3** **Read the email and correct the mistakes. There are 8 mistakes.**

Example I had the ~~baddest~~ ^{worst} cold I've ever had in my life.

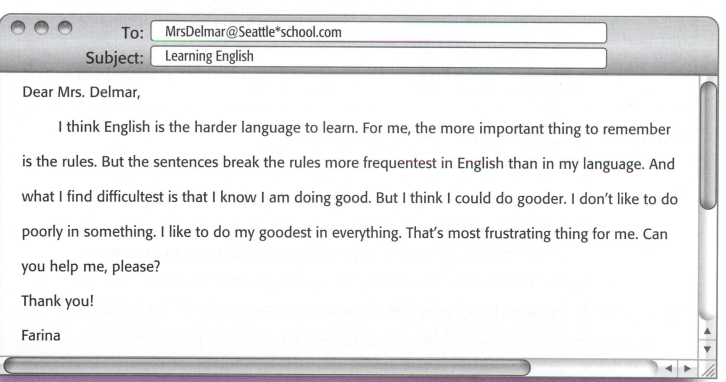

To: MrsDelmar@Seattle*school.com

Subject: Learning English

Dear Mrs. Delmar,

I think English is the harder language to learn. For me, the more important thing to remember

is the rules. But the sentences break the rules more frequentest in English than in my language. And

what I find difficultest is that I know I am doing good. But I think I could do gooder. I don't like to do

poorly in something. I like to do my goodest in everything. That's most frustrating thing for me. Can

you help me, please?

Thank you!

Farina

Practice 63 Superlatives

EXAMPLE	EXPLANATION
Michael Jordan was **the most popular** athlete in the world. He became one of **the richest** people in the world. For many years, he was **the most valuable** player.	We use the superlative form to point out the number 1 item in a group of two or more.

Language Notes: 1. Use *the* before a superlative form. Omit *the* if there is a possessive form before the superlative form:

Jack is *my* tallest friend.

2. We sometimes put a prepositional phrase at the end of a superlative sentence:

in the world   in my family   in my class   in my country

3. We sometimes say *one of the* before a superlative form. Then we use a plural noun:

He was *one of the best athletes* in the world.

4. An adjective clause with *ever* and the present perfect tense often complete a superlative statement:

Michael Jordan is one of the best athletes *who has ever lived.*

■ EXERCISE 1   Complete the sentence with a superlative adjective from the box.

Example The Sears Tower is one of the _____tallest_____ buildings in the world.

~~tallest~~	easiest	wisest	rarest	largest	fastest
worst	silliest	shortest	greatest	smallest	

1. Gandhi was one of the _____ people who ever lived.

2. The snow leopard is one of the _____ animals in the world.

3. February is the _____ month in the year.

4. Jupiter is the _____ planet.

5. Comedies can be the _____ kinds of movies.

6. Picasso was one of the _____ painters of the 20th century.

7. The cheetah is the _____ animal on four legs.

8. Email is one of the _____ forms of communication.

■ EXERCISE 2   Answer the question with a complete sentence.

Example Q: What is the most beautiful city in your country?

A: I think Madrid is the most beautiful city in my country.

1. Q: What animal do you think is the most intelligent?

A: _____

2. Q: When did you meet your best friend?

A: _____

3. Q: Who is the happiest person that you know?

A: _____

4. Q: What is the saddest movie that you've ever seen?

A: _____

■ **EXERCISE 3** Read the Web page and correct the mistakes. There are 10 mistakes.

Example I just watched the ~~funnier~~ *funniest* movie ever!

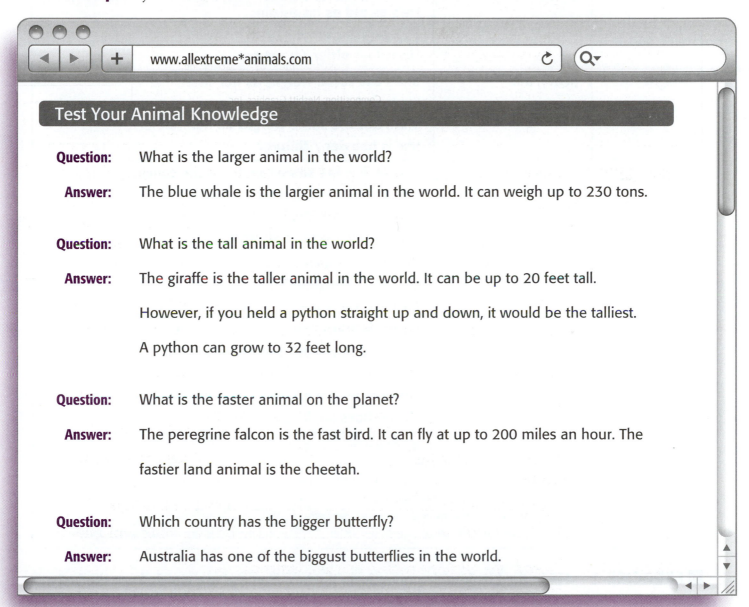

www.allextreme*animals.com

Test Your Animal Knowledge

Question: What is the larger animal in the world?

Answer: The blue whale is the largier animal in the world. It can weigh up to 230 tons.

Question: What is the tall animal in the world?

Answer: The giraffe is the taller animal in the world. It can be up to 20 feet tall.

However, if you held a python straight up and down, it would be the talliest.

A python can grow to 32 feet long.

Question: What is the faster animal on the planet?

Answer: The peregrine falcon is the fast bird. It can fly at up to 200 miles an hour. The

fastier land animal is the cheetah.

Question: Which country has the bigger butterfly?

Answer: Australia has one of the biggust butterflies in the world.

Practice 64 Equality and Difference with Nouns and Adjectives

NOUN	ADJECTIVE	EXAMPLE
height	tall, short	He's **the same height as** his wife. He's **as tall as** his wife. He's **not the same height as** his brother. His brother is **taller / shorter**.
age	old, young	He's **the same age as** his cousin. He's **as old as** his cousin. He's **not the same age as** his wife. His wife is **older / younger**.
weight	heavy, thin	She's **the same weight as** her sister. She's **as heavy as** her sister. She's **not the same weight as** her mother. She is **heavier / thinner**.
length	long, short	This shelf is **the same length as** the couch. This shelf is **as long as** the couch. This shelf is **not the same length as** the rug. This shelf is **longer / shorter**.
price	expensive, cheap	My car is **the same price as** your car. My car is **as expensive as** your car. My car is **not the same price as** her car. My car is **more expensive / cheaper**.
size	big, small	These shoes are **the same size as** those sneakers. These shoes are **as big as** those sneakers. These shoes are **not the same size as** those sandals. These shoes are **bigger / smaller**.

Language Notes: 1. For equality with nouns, use *the same . . . as*:
   She's *the same age as* her husband.
2. For equality with adjectives and adverbs, use *as . . . as*:
   She's *as old as* her husband.
3. For difference with nouns, use *not the same . . . as*:
   She's *not the same age as* her sister.   (She and her sister are *not the same age.*)

■ **EXERCISE 1**   Fill in the blank with a noun from the box. You can use words from the box more than once.

Example A yard is about the same _____ length _____ as a meter.

height	age	weight	length	price	size

1. Your new car is almost the same _____ as your apartment!

2. She has a teacher who is the same _____ as her father.

3. Do you have a better computer that's about the same _____ as this one?

4. You're growing so fast that you're the same _____ as your older sister now.

5. I need a box that's about the same _____ as this gift so I can mail it.

■ **EXERCISE 2** **Read the sentence. Then write a second sentence that means the same thing, using *not as . . . as*.**

Example The highway is wider than the road.

<u>The road isn't as wide as the highway.</u>_____

1. The Netherlands is flatter than Switzerland.

_____

2. Switzerland is more mountainous than the Netherlands.

_____

3. He's friendlier than his roommate.

_____

4. Your teacher is more helpful than mine.

_____

5. This movie was more interesting than the last one we saw.

_____

■ **EXERCISE 3** **Read the conversation and correct the mistakes. There are 7 mistakes.**

Example I can type ~~fastest~~ *faster* than you can.

Jacques: This blue bicycle is as expensiver as the red one.

François: But it's not costly as the yellow one we saw yesterday.

Jacques: Yes, it's cheaper the yellow one.

François: It costs the same the green one we looked at last week.

Jacques: I don't want to buy a bicycle that is expensive as the blue one.

François: Do you want to buy one that is as expensive the yellow one?

Jacques: No. I want a green one that is the cheaper.

Practice 65 Overview of the Passive Voice

EXAMPLE	EXPLANATION
The fire **was started** by a careless camper.	The passive verb uses a form of *be* + the past participle.
Many trees **were burned**.	The passive voice is used when the subject receives the action of the verb.
The fire **will be put out by the rangers**.	Sometimes the performer of the action is included after a passive verb. Use *by* + noun / object pronoun for the performer.
Some homes **were burned**.	Usually the performer is not included in a passive sentence.

Language Note: The verb in a passive voice sentence shows that the subject receives the action. The verb in an active voice sentence shows that the subject performs the action of the verb.
Active: The cat *ate* the mouse. → Passive: The mouse *was eaten* by the cat.

■ EXERCISE 1   Underline the verb. Identify the sentence as *passive* or *active*.

Example Our friend Kathy <u>may not be accepted</u> to the university. _____*passive*_____

1. Radium was discovered by Marie Curie. _____

2. Jesse is finishing up the project right now. _____

3. You ought to be examined by a specialist. _____

4. These beautiful carpets are made entirely by hand. _____

5. The new office building is being built by the McArthur Company.
   _____

6. The winners of the Nobel Prizes will be announced later this week.
   _____

7. Everyone enjoyed the camping trip. _____

8. One of the pieces of the puzzle was lost. _____

9. I cook breakfast for my family every morning. _____

10. Corn is grown in Kansas. _____

■ EXERCISE 2   ⟲Circle⟳ the correct passive form. Write who did the action at the end of the statement.

Example Tonight's news <u>sponsors</u> / ⟲<u>is sponsored</u>⟳ by the ACME Corporation.
   <u>by the ACME Corporation</u>

1. The First National Bank <u>was robbed / robbed</u> this afternoon around 3 o'clock by two robbers.
   _____

2. The robbers <u>has not been caught</u> / <u>have not been caught</u> yet.
_____

3. Six firefighters <u>were taked</u> / <u>were taken</u> out of a forest fire 50 miles east of here.
_____

4. They <u>were brought</u> / <u>were brung</u> to the hospital for second-degree burns.
_____

5. All roads in the area <u>has been closed</u> / <u>have been closed</u> to everyone except the firefighters.
_____

6. A new mayor <u>elected</u> / <u>was elected</u>.
_____

7. Results of the election <u>were announced</u> / <u>was announced</u> just an hour ago.
_____

8. A conference on disease <u>is being hold</u> / <u>is being held</u> this week at the Medical Center.
_____

9. A new drug to fight the disease <u>have been study</u> / <u>has been studied</u> by researchers at our medical school.
_____

10. The research project <u>was starting</u> / <u>was started</u> by a group of international corporations.
_____

■ **EXERCISE 3** **Read the paragraph. Change the sentences that use the passive voice to sentences that use the active voice. 4 sentences need to be changed.**

Example *I filled a glass of water from the faucet.*
~~A glass of water was filled from the faucet.~~

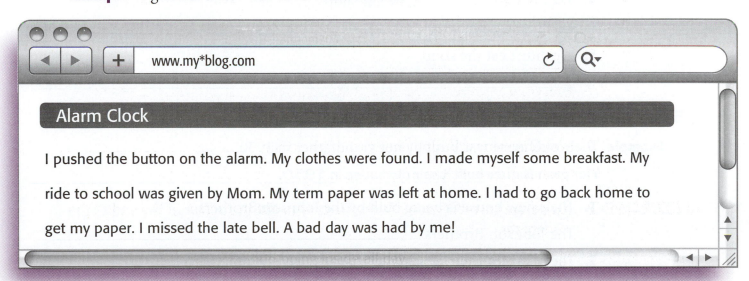

Alarm Clock

I pushed the button on the alarm. My clothes were found. I made myself some breakfast. My ride to school was given by Mom. My term paper was left at home. I had to go back home to get my paper. I missed the late bell. A bad day was had by me!

TENSE	ACTIVE	PASSIVE (*BE* + PAST PARTICPLE)
Simple present	They **take** a vote.	A vote **is taken**.
Simple past	They **took** a vote.	A vote **was taken**.
Future	They **will take** a vote.	A vote **will be taken**.
Present continuous	They **are going to take** a vote.	A vote **is going to be taken**.
Present perfect	They **have taken** a vote.	A vote **has been taken**.
Modal	They **must take** a vote.	A vote **must be taken**.

■ **EXERCISE 1** Change the sentence from active to passive. Do not include a performer. (Do not include *by* + the performer.)

Examples They could build a new house. <u>A new house could be built.</u>

She drank orange juice. <u>Orange juice was drunk.</u>

1. They planned their vacation carefully.

   _____

2. When will you finish your composition?

   _____

3. I can't change the tire here.

   _____

4. They bought T-shirts at the gift shop.

   _____

5. We didn't eat the soup.

   _____

■ **EXERCISE 2** Change the sentence from passive to active.

Example Their old house was built by her grandfather in 1930.

Her grandfather <u>built their old house in 1930.</u>

1. Their new house is being built by the Johnson Brothers.

   The Johnson Brothers _____.

2. The plans for their new garden haven't been completed yet.

   They _____.

3. Trees, flowers, and grass will have to be planted after the house is completed. They _____.

4. The mortgage must be repaid within 30 years.

They _____.

5. Their new house was designed by their oldest daughter.

Their oldest daughter _____.

■ **EXERCISE 3** **Write a passive sentence for the subject.**

Example The Eiffel Tower <u>was built in the 19th century.</u>

1. The cat _____.

2. My grades _____.

3. The food _____.

4. My car _____.

5. My computer _____.

■ **EXERCISE 4** **Read the paragraph and correct the mistakes. There are 8 mistakes.**

Example The store ~~opened~~ *was opened* in 1898.

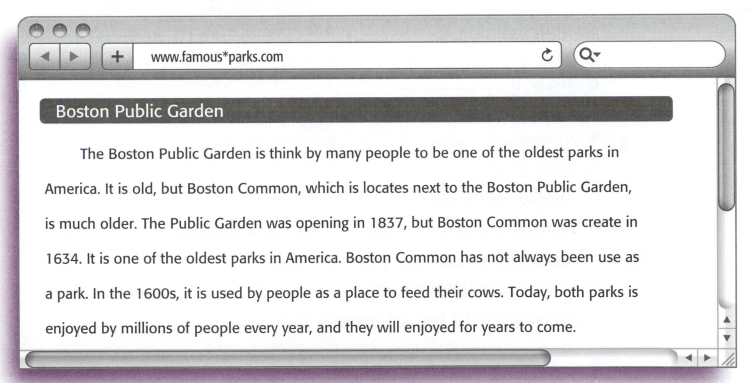

Boston Public Garden

The Boston Public Garden is think by many people to be one of the oldest parks in America. It is old, but Boston Common, which is locates next to the Boston Public Garden, is much older. The Public Garden was opening in 1837, but Boston Common was create in 1634. It is one of the oldest parks in America. Boston Common has not always been use as a park. In the 1600s, it is used by people as a place to feed their cows. Today, both parks is enjoyed by millions of people every year, and they will enjoyed for years to come.

Classifying or Identifying the Subject with the Indefinite Article

EXAMPLE	EXPLANATION
A tent is a shelter that is used by campers. Electricity was **an** important invention in the 19th century.	We use the indefinite articles *a* and *an* to classify or identify the subject of a sentence.
Passports are official documents used by travelers. My parents are bank workers.	When we classify a plural subject, we don't use any article at all.

Language Note: When we classify or identify the subject, we are telling who or what the subject is:
What is *a* hammer? A hammer is *a* tool.
Who was Albert Einstein? He was *a* great physicist.

■ **EXERCISE 1** Match each question with its answer.

1. Dew is _____*a*_____
2. A watch is _____
3. A map is _____
4. Pineapples are _____
5. Farmers are _____
6. An alarm is _____
7. Tourists are _____
8. A lifeguard is _____
9. Forest rangers are _____
10. A ruler is _____

a. water on the grass in the morning.
b. a device for measuring things.
c. people who take care of forests.
d. a device that sounds a warning.
e. a drawing that shows where things are.
f. vacationers who are sightseeing.
g. a person who saves swimmers in danger.
h. people who grow crops to sell them.
i. a device that tells time.
j. tropical fruit.

■ **EXERCISE 2** Correct the sentence by adding *a* or *an* where it is needed.

Example Omelet is dish made with eggs.

  <u>An omelet is a dish made with eggs.</u>

1. Bird is animal that flies and lays eggs.

  _____

2. Gasoline is fuel that is made from petroleum.

  _____

3. Train is form of public transportation.

  _____

4. Match is small stick of wood or paper that is used to start fire.

  _____

5. Stove is appliance that is used to cook food in kitchen.

_____

6. Kitchen is room where people prepare their food.

_____

7. Glue is liquid that is used to stick things together.

_____

8. Scanner is electronic device that can copy pictures and words.

_____

◼ EXERCISE 3   **Write a sentence that classifies, identifies, or defines the word. Use the proper form of the verb _be_.**

Example A tablecloth _is a cloth that is used to cover a table._ _____

1. A door _____.

2. A planet _____.

3. Volcanoes _____.

4. Pets _____.

5. A truck _____.

◼ EXERCISE 4   **Read the conversation and correct the mistakes. There are 10 mistakes.**

Example Horses are ~~a~~ good ~~animal~~ ^{animals} for riding.

Raj: What is a lantern?

Faisal: A lantern is a type of lights. A lanterns are often used when camping.

Lanterns run on batteries or gas, and not by electricity.

Raj: What is a batteries?

Faisal: Battery is a way of getting electricity. Batteries don't need to be plugged

into a wall outlet. Battery can be found in cell phone, in flashlights, and

in a toys.

Raj: What is flashlight?

Faisal: Flashlight is another way of getting light. Flashlights can be held in your

hand and used to light the way in front of you. A flashlights is a good

thing to have at home when the electricity goes out.

	SINGULAR COUNT	PLURAL COUNT	NONCOUNT
Affirmative	We need **a** new tent. I'm taking **an** umbrella.	We'll need (**some**) matches.	Let's take (**some**) drinking water.
Negative	Don't bring **a** hair dryer.	We won't need (**any**) napkins.	We don't have (**any**) ice.
Question	Will there be **a** picnic table?	Did you pack (**any**) cups and plates?	Will there be (**any**) firewood for sale?

Language Notes: 1. We use *a* or *an* to introduce a singular count noun into the conversation. We use *some* or *any* to introduce a noncount noun or a plural count noun into the conversation.

2. *Some* and *any* can be omitted:
I don't have *any* time to help you.
I don't have (Ø) time to help you.

■ **EXERCISE 1**   Complete the sentence with *a, an, any,* or *some.*

Example Do you want _____*a*_____ donut?

1. Do you have _____ sugar?

2. He will need _____ new notebook for his new class.

3. She bought _____ beautiful ceramic vase at the antique store.

4. Your teacher won't teach _____ pronunciation course next semester.

5. The thirsty children want _____ lemonade.

6. My family rode the subway to _____ wonderful restaurant.

7. The car doesn't have _____ gas right now. Sorry.

8. Did he have _____ toothpaste in his suitcase?

9. _____ picnic is _____ outdoor meal.

10. _____ bird doesn't have _____ teeth, so it never needs a dentist.

■ **EXERCISE 2**   Answer the question using *a, an, any,* or *some.*

Example Q: What do people sometimes drink in the morning to give them vitamins?

A: People sometimes drink some orange juice in the morning to get some vitamins.

1. **Q:** What can't you take on an airplane?

   A: _____

2. **Q:** What should you not forget to do before a car trip?

   A: _____

3. Q: What should you take when you go shopping?

A: _____

4. Q: What do you always keep in your refrigerator?

A: _____

5. Q: What do you usually eat for breakfast?

A: _____

6. Q: What did you buy the last time you went shopping?

A: _____

7. Q: What do you need to bring to class?

A: _____

8. Q: What do you need to make a cake?

A: _____

■ **EXERCISE 3   Read the email and correct the mistakes. There are 9 mistakes.**

Example I got͜letter in the mail today.
_(a)_

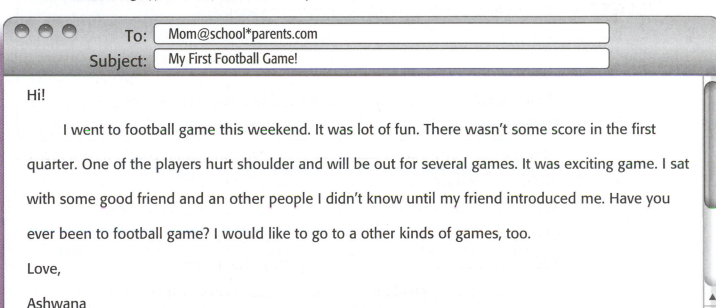

To: Mom@school*parents.com

Subject: My First Football Game!

Hi!

    I went to football game this weekend. It was lot of fun. There wasn't some score in the first

quarter. One of the players hurt shoulder and will be out for several games. It was exciting game. I sat

with some good friend and an other people I didn't know until my friend introduced me. Have you

ever been to football game? I would like to go to a other kinds of games, too.

Love,

Ashwana

Practice 69 Definite Articles

EXAMPLE	EXPLANATION
The bank gives you **a** personal identification number. You should memorize **the** number.	A noun is first introduced as an indefinite noun. When referring to it again, the definite article (*the*) is used.
Would you please get **the** milk out of **the** refrigerator?	The speaker is speaking to a person or an object that is present.
There are many problems in **the** world.	There is only one in our experience.
Where's **the** teacher? I have a question about **the** homework.	The speaker and the listener share a common experience. Students in the same class talk about **the** teacher, **the** homework, **the** board.
I spent **the** money you gave me.	The speaker defines or specifies exactly which one.
I went to **the** store for some groceries. I stopped by **the** bank to get some cash.	We often use *the* with certain familiar places and people when we refer to the one that we usually use: the bank the beach the bus the doctor the post office the train the park the hospital the store

Language Note: We use the definite article (*the*) when the speaker and the listener have the same person(s) or objects(s) in mind. The listener knows exactly what the speaker is referring to as in the examples above.

■ **EXERCISE 1** Read the paragraph. Then fill in the blanks with *a, an,* or *the*.

Example Yesterday I decided to find _____*an*_____ apartment to rent.

      I bought (1) _____ newspaper and found (2) _____ advertisement for (3) _____ one-bedroom apartment. It sounded perfect! So I called (4) _____ number in the paper. (5) _____ landlord answered and told me about (6) _____ apartment. I met (7) _____ landlord at (8) _____ apartment today so that I could have a look at it. I liked (9) _____ living room, but (10) _____ bedroom was a little small. I decided to take it anyway. (11) _____ apartment isn't furnished, so I need to get some furniture. Fortunately, I already have (12) _____ table and (13) _____ armchair. I will have to buy (14) _____ bed. I don't want to sleep on (15) _____ floor!

■ **EXERCISE 2** Fill in the blanks with *a, an, the, some,* or *any*.

Example We took _____*a*_____ vacation. _____*The*_____ vacation was wonderful.

   1. Every morning, _____ sun woke us up as it came through _____ eastern window of _____ little cabin we rented.

2. We made _____ good breakfast and drank _____ hot coffee with it.

3. There wasn't _____ telephone or _____ television in the cabin.

4. For entertainment, we took _____ long walks in the woods.

5. We had _____ good conversations too.

6. Every day after lunch, we wrote _____ postcards to our friends.

7. Then we mailed _____ postcards at _____ post office.

8. In _____ evening, we watched _____ moon rise.

9. We didn't feel _____ stress _____ whole time we were there.

10. We still talk about _____ wonderful time that we had together.

■ **EXERCISE 3** **Unscramble the words to write a correct sentence.**

Example a / the / the / map / city / telephone book / find / of / can / you / in

<u>You can find a map of the city in the telephone book.</u>_____

1. teacher / we will have / substitute / so / a / teacher / the / is sick today

_____

2. go to / at / look / zoo / bears / let's / the / the / and

_____

3. to listen / like / rain / roof / on / the / the / I / to

_____

4. dictionary / I / need / that I / to replace / lost / the

_____

■ **EXERCISE 4** **Read the paragraph and correct the mistakes. There are 10 mistakes.**

Example I checked $\overset{the}{\wedge}$ term paper before $\overset{the}{\wedge}$ next bell rang.

A Good Vacation

When we got to border between the United States and Canada, the guards asked us to stop car. We

had to show guards our passports. We had to tell guards why we were going to Canada. We told the guards

that we wanted to see Niagara Falls. We had to get out of car so guards could look under car. We got back

in car and went to waterfall. It was one of best vacations ever!

Practice 70   Indefinite Pronouns

DEFINITE PRONOUN	INDEFINITE PRONOUN
My daughter has a new doll. Do you want to see **it**?	My daughter has a new doll. Her friend has **one** too.
My friend got money from his grandparents. He wants to spend **it**.	He got money for his birthday. You got **some** too. Did you get **any** for your graduation?
I have a young son. I take **him** to the park every day.	I have a son. Do you have **one**?
My son has some video games. He likes to play with **them**.	My son has some video games. Does your son have **any**?

Language Notes:
1. We use definite pronouns (*him, her, it, them*) to refer to definite count nouns.
2. We use *one* to refer to an indefinite singular count noun.
3. We use *some* (for statements) and *any* (for negatives and questions) to refer to an indefinite noncount noun or an indefinite plural count noun.
4. We can use *any* and *some* before *more*.

■ **EXERCISE 1**   Read the sentence. Then fill in the blanks with an indefinite pronoun (*some, any,* or *one*) or a definite pronoun (*them* or *it*).

Example I had a DVD player, but I spilled _____some_____ tea on it, and now _____it_____ doesn't work.

1. I either need to get _____ repaired or buy a new _____.

2. I saw an ad for a used _____ in the campus newspaper.

3. Maybe my parents will give me _____ for my birthday.

4. They cost a lot of money, and right now I don't have _____.

5. My neighbor has two. He uses _____ to watch movies.

6. Maybe he'd lend me _____ until I can buy _____.

7. I could return _____ to him whenever he needs _____.

8. He had three DVD players, but he gave _____ to his daughter last month.

■ **EXERCISE 2**   Answer the question. Substitute an indefinite pronoun (*one, some,* or *any*) or a definite pronoun (*it* or *them*) for the underlined words.

Example Do you like <u>scary movies</u>?

<u>No, I don't like them.</u>

1. Do you have <u>a bus pass</u>?

_____

2. Where do you do <u>your grocery shopping</u>?

_____

3. How often do you write <u>letters</u> to your family?

_____

4. Do you have <u>any gum</u> with you?

_____

5. Do you have <u>a computer</u>?

_____

6. Did you download <u>any songs</u> this week?

_____

■ **EXERCISE 3**   **Write a response for the question using *some, any, one, them,* or *it*.**

Example Q: Is there an elevator in this building?

   A: <u>Yes, there's one next to the restroom.</u>

1. Q: Have you ever ridden a bus in this city?

   A: _____

2. Q: Did you have any pets when you were younger?

   A: _____

3. Q: Where's the nearest bookstore?

   A: _____

■ **EXERCISE 4**   **Read the email and correct the mistakes. There are 7 mistakes.**

Example My sister does not have ~~some~~ ^{any} boyfriends.

To: Sonja@My*Pen*Pal.com

Subject: I am Mei Hua Chen

Hello Sonja,

   My name is Mei Hua Chen. I have a brother, but I am older than it. Do you have some? I like to

go to the movies at the movie theater near my house. Do you have it where you live? When I go to the

movies, I like to eat popcorn. I always want any more popcorn when I finish mine! I like to eat candy,

but my mother doesn't let me eat some at the movie theater. I can only have any at home. I'm excited

to have a pen pal. I've never had some before!

Your friend,

Mei Hua Chen

More Grammar Practice 2, Second Edition

Publisher: Sherrise Roehr

Managing Development Editor: John Hicks

Acquisitions Editor: Tom Jefferies

Director of U.S. Marketing: Jim McDonough

Marketing Manager: Caitlin Driscoll

Manufacturing Manager: Marcia Locke

Manufacturing Buyer: Marybeth Hennebury

Director of Content and Media Production:
   Michael Burggren

Content Project Manager: Daisy Sosa

Cover Design: Muse Group, Inc.

Cover Image: Yanie, eps10 vector background,
   shutterstock.com

Composition: Nesbitt Graphics, Inc.

Interior Design: Muse Group, Inc.

ISBN-13: 978-1-111-22042-6

ISBN-10: 1-111-22042-5

Heinle
20 Channel Center Street
Boston, MA 02210
USA

Cengage Learning is a leading provider of customized learning solutions with office locations around the globe, including Singapore, the United Kingdom, Australia, Mexico, Brazil, and Japan. Locate your local office at: **international.cengage.com/region**

Cengage Learning products are represented in Canada by Nelson Education, Ltd.

Visit Heinle online at **elt.heinle.com**
Visit our corporate website at **www.cengage.com**

Printed in the United States of America
7 8 9 10 11   21 20 19 18 17